Empowered Co-Parenting With A Narcissistic-Ex

Setting Boundaries, Ensuring Clear Communication, Understanding the Narcissist and Practicing Self-Care

Harmony Fielding

Table of Contents

Introduction

You yourself, as much as anybody in the entire universe, deserve your love and affection. –Buddha

Changing the nature of any relationship, especially a toxic one, requires determination, courage, and self-discipline. Pulling the rug from under the narcissist's feet takes great inner strength. Well done for digging deep within yourself and finding the strength to prioritize your well-being.

By choosing to leave a relationship marred with narcissistic abuse, you boldly prioritized your and your kids' well-being. Celebrate because you saw beyond the illusions of the narcissist and, despite all, decided to live your very best life.

Women trapped in narcissistic relationships often carry tremendous responsibilities, and these women usually face challenges at home and work. Always trying to fix problems, keep the peace, and maintain a stable home life all alone is a considerable weight.

There is often a "smoke and mirrors" approach to the way in which a narcissist abandons their family. While the narcissist is at home, their priorities and focus are elsewhere. Unfortunately, it is left up to the woman to make some difficult decisions when this happens. When the woman has tried alone and failed alone to pick up the pieces of a broken relationship, it is heartbreaking to be the one who finally decides to break the family up.

The most effective way to ensure a response from a narcissist is to remove them from their chaotic comfort zones and confront them alongside a team of professionals. Once you realize how quickly a coward backs down, you'll realize that the only way forward with them is to maintain a no-strings-attached, business-like relationship.

Women work hard to ensure that their home is where everyone in the family unit wants to be. Sadly, when you are living with a narcissist, this is not possible. Like many people, Rachel is a good example of someone who learned to her detriment that bad situations get worse over time, not better.

Rachel had always wondered how and why women stayed in toxic relationships until she became one of those women. She never expected to become trapped in a poisonous relationship herself. Neither had she anticipated the long-term damage that being in a relationship with a narcissist would cause.

In her late twenties, Rachel decided to make some life-changing decisions, one of which was moving to a new country. While the change was exciting, she found that cultural differences conflicted with her beliefs and values.

Rachel had had enough loving relationships before moving to notice that the dynamics of her romantic relationships in her newfound home were very different. Despite this, Rachel met Richard, a charming and seemingly confident man with similar interests. Richard ticked all Rachel's boxes, and the timing of their meeting was ideal. Their relationship developed quickly, and Rachel soon fell in love with Richard.

Their relationship started quite well, but Rachel noticed some disturbing red flags not too long into the relationship. She became increasingly aware that Richard was not overly concerned about her feelings and was rather self-absorbed.

In instances where Rachel thought Richard's behavior was insensitive, if not callous, she overlooked this, wondering if she was perhaps being oversensitive. Richard increasingly ignored Rachel's feelings, going as far as ignoring her in public and often showing an active interest in other women.

Eventually, things became so challenging that the couple no longer even went out to dinner together because of his behavior. A lot of important issues that needed to be addressed were overlooked, and Rachel's feelings were swept under the rug.

At almost 40, Rachel's life felt like a never-ending rollercoaster ride, which kept her busy and distracted. Guilt trips, accusations, lies, gaslighting, blame-shifting, and arguments became an almost daily occurrence.

Nothing ever seemed to change, no matter how much Rachel tried to explain her feelings and views on issues. Rachel often sidestepped issues, resolving some, but most were left unresolved, suspended in mid-air.

The more problems Rachel seemed to resolve, the more Richard brought to the door. Rachel became so busy trying to solve issues that she never took the time to stand back and take stock of where her life was heading.

Perplexed, she could not understand the explosivity of their relationship. Despite everything, Rachel felt she could not end her relationship with Richard; instead, she stayed committed, believing it was too late to start over.

After ten challenging years and the birth of two beautiful kids, life was not easy, and an accumulation of unresolved frustrations left Rachel feeling angry and drained. Rachel had invested a lot of time and energy trying to rationalize with Richard and found that no approach worked with him. It was simply impossible to get the message across.

Despite Rachel's everyday difficulties, more bad news was to come. This news would lead her to finally choose herself and her kids over everything else. When Rachel found out that she had cancer, her life changed drastically. While one would think her first concern would be ridding herself of cancer, this was not the case.

Suddenly, it was as if she had become painfully aware of everything fundamentally wrong in her life. The harsh reality concerning her quality of life instantly came to the forefront.

Finally, Rachel knew that she had no choice but to address all of the issues that had been swept under the carpet for so long. She realized she could no longer sacrifice her health and happiness; and that many things in her life needed to change. No longer could she accept being a sufferer or victim of anything, not cancer and definitely not narcissistic abuse.

Realizing there was no way to save her relationship with Richard, Rachel knew it was time to go. It broke her heart to split her family up, but it was the only way for her and her kids to live a healthier, more wholesome life.

As if a bright light bulb suddenly lit up, Rachel realized that holding onto any anger and hurt would only make her bitter from the inside out. Sadly, this bitterness would affect her health even more and rob her kids of an emotionally mature and stable parent.

Without a shadow of a doubt, Rachel knew that she did not want to spend another ten years with a narcissist. She became painfully aware that it was not only her who was suffering but her kids as well. The kids were now old enough, and they would be able to handle their parents' separation.

After leaving Richard, Rachel suddenly found that she had more space for herself, and she regretted accepting narcissistic abuse for so long and not acting sooner. It was enlightening for her to see that peace and joy had been only one decision and step away. Moreover, Rachel realized her story and knowledge could help others going through a similar journey.

Narcissism is a personality disorder that affects far more people than we realize. Sadly, the damages of narcissistic personality disorder are not limited to the sufferer but to their unsuspecting victims. Shockingly enough, Bree Bonchay, the founder of World Narcissistic Abuse Day, stated that in the United States alone, up to 158 million people are currently affected by narcissistic abuse (Mohsin, 2022).

The sad reality is that countless people worldwide spend years repairing the devastating damages caused by narcissistic abuse. Narcissism profoundly impacts people of all ages, genders, religions, and cultures. Unfortunately, once you have been the victim of a narcissist, you can be sure that your life and how you see the world will change as a result.

Narcissists pride themselves on playing the game of one-upmanship on others. If a narcissist cannot bring you down to their level, they will compete to be better than you. This book aims to help you implement a set of behaviors where a narcissist will fight to be the best parent they can be.

No one person on the planet is perfect; we can all make mistakes and choices that we regret later in life. At the very least, making "mistakes" give us an opportunity to learn and grow from them.

While some choices you may have made could have gone against your values and rules, it forces you to question and evaluate who you truly are. Learning from your mistakes allows you the opportunity to do better in the future and provides pathways to emotional growth.

Drama, emotional rollercoasters, and trauma were a part of your world for so long that you became a shadow of the person you once were. In the past, anxiety, depression, and fear may have nearly consumed you alive.

So many times, you felt like you were being pushed to your limits. Yet no matter how difficult things became, you always chose to strive onward and upward. To have overcome all that you did, you are a powerful force.

Remember, you are not alone, and your life is certainly not over; it has only just begun. Not only will you and your kids survive, but you will also thrive and achieve great things. Despite everything, your kids will grow up to be well-balanced, kind, considerate, and confident adults.

You will rise above and change your attitude toward your narcissistic ex to create a more peaceful and productive co-parenting relationship. No longer will you just put up with bad behavior.

A new beginning lies ahead where you are so empowered that a narcissist's drama and manipulations no longer affect you. You will learn to avoid endless arguments and conflict and harness the narcissist's needs for your and your kids' best interests. Soon your life will be bigger than the narcissist, and you will not be tempted to return to him.

While there were likely times when you have wondered if you would ever enjoy a peaceful, happy, healthy life, the great news is that you can and will. In the not-too-distant future, you will be at a place where your narcissistic ex does not consume your thoughts. Setting healthy boundaries will help you deal with the toxic behavior of your ex.

Many people believe that once you have left a toxic relationship, things in your life naturally return to normal, and this is not the truth. The real work begins once you have finally closed the door on the relationship.

This book contains tried, tested, and proven steps to help you transform an negative, disruptive relationship into a more beneficial one. The guidelines outlined can help you establish a functional and healthy co-parenting relationship with your ex. From here on out, you will stay disciplined and focused on your kid's well-being and interact with your ex on a whole new level.

As a mother, you want to raise emotionally stable and mature kids who respect themselves and others. Your kids need you to be their anchor through the storms of life.

You are the loving, guiding light in a potentially dark tunnel for your kids. Instead of having regrets, see this experience as a trigger to motivate you to step out of your comfort zone and become someone you never dared to be.

Well done for being prepared to set boundaries, ensure clear communication, understand the narcissist, and practice self-care. It is now time to let the healing work begin, to put your focus on your kids, and to avoid conflict with your narcissistic ex. Let's leap in and start by looking at how you can regain complete control of your life and begin to wipe the slate clean.

Chapter 1:

Wipe the Slate Clean

You are the master of your own destiny. Use your strengths well. They are the keys to your destiny and your success in life. –Gautama Buddha

Each new day you wake up is a chance for you to do better than you did the previous day. With every new day comes the fantastic opportunity to change and become the person you want to be deep down inside you. You can choose to and have the power to evolve into a stronger and more enlightened person. The ability to change your life lies in your hands and your hands alone.

You can shape your life into whatever you choose and create your success. Choose to focus on your strengths and use them wisely so that you can powerfully overcome any obstacles and achieve the goals you have set for yourself. Be bold, be courageous, and decide that today offers you a new chance to grow, live and learn. Affirm that today is a day created for you to achieve, believe and dream.

Life can be particularly chaotic when you share your life with a narcissist. It is normal that ongoing chaos and drama will drain you, stretch you to your limits, and test you in crazy ways. It does not matter how strong and resilient you may think you are; sharing your life with a narcissist is not for the faint-hearted.

A narcissist will test every boundary that you have. To the outside world, they will quite easily portray themselves as victims. However, behind closed doors, they will act like the enemy and choose to do the exact opposite of what you want.

Their manipulations can be confusing. They will quite easily give you the impression that they have agreed with you when they do not. The truth is the narcissist will invest a lot of time subtly provoking, mocking, humiliating, pushing boundaries, and creating all sorts of chaos.

Once you finally call a halt to their perverted circus and they no longer live with you, cutting ties and setting healthy boundaries becomes far easier. This chapter will explore cutting physical, emotional, and financial ties with a narcissist.

Imposing Physical Boundaries

It can be challenging to avoid contact with your narcissistic ex, who you are trying to co-parent with, but there are instances where you may have to do it. Dealing with a co-parent who is a narcissist can be frustrating, daunting, and even dangerous at times. There are instances where completely avoiding contact is the only option for your peace of mind and your kids' protection.

Cutting ties with your narcissistic ex will involve removing anything linked to them. One of the first ways you can cut physical ties with your ex is by moving into your own home. Once you have managed to do this, you do not have to give your ex access to your house. Your home is your sanctuary and safe place. If you really do not want certain people in your home, then you do not allow them in. When there are any changeovers involving your kids, ensure these exchanges are outside your building or front door.

When you start working on avoiding contact with your narcissistic ex, cut down on physically interacting with them. Avoid events or occasions where you may encounter them. Remove or at least limit their physical presence from your life. You and your kids will be filling this gap by becoming the main priorities in your life. You will no longer have to endure the narcissist's incessant jostling for attention. This will give you a clean break and the necessary headspace to start afresh.

Cutting Emotional Ties

When a relationship with a narcissistic ex ends, while it can often come as a huge relief, moving on and finding closure can be tricky when you have kids together.

Attitude

Your attitude determines your altitude, and adopting an entirely new attitude toward your narcissistic ex is key. Your ex is no longer your husband or lover, and he will understand this by how you treat him. The first step is to start treating your ex in a more neutral manner.

How you communicate with your ex will convey whether or not you mean business and whether or not you are willing to accept their manipulative tactics. With the correct attitude, they will soon realize that, in a sense, their behavior no longer affects you on an emotional level.

When co-parenting with your ex, ensure that all your communication is:

- formal

- intentional

- professional

- unemotional

Formal communication with your narcissistic ex might feel a bit like playing a game of advanced mental chess. However, in this game, you are the only one strategizing while the narcissist moves the pieces around the board randomly.

When talking to a narcissist, be mindful to choose your words carefully so as not to give them any ammunition they can use against you.

Anticipate their possible reactions, like deflecting responsibility or trying to bring you back into their negative narcissistic sphere.

The chances are good that the narcissist might not have listened to a single word you were saying, even if you have thoughtfully communicated. Instead, the narcissist might go on a self-important rant and blame you for any or all of the problems that they are facing. Stand firm and confident in your beliefs and values.

It is understandable to feel belittled and frustrated when the narcissist speaks to you in a manipulative way. However, remember to stay strong and protect yourself from their self-centered charm. Do not for one-second doubt yourself, and always prioritize your well-being.

Communicate only with intention while being smart and strategic. Keep your goals in mind and choose your battles with the narcissist wisely. Be mindful to only focus on matters directly related to the kids. Always maintain your boundaries and keep a record of everything.

When communicating with a narcissistic ex-partner, always remain focused on the matter at hand and avoid becoming sucked into personal attacks. Keep your boundaries clear and maintain a calm and professional demeanor at all times. Do not allow the narcissist a gap where they can sidetrack the conversation with subtle insults.

Keep your feelings in check and avoid giving them any ammunition to use against you later. Stick to the facts, avoid personal attacks, and focus on practical matters. Remember to remain patient, resilient, and assertive because, armed with these traits, you can successfully unemotionally communicate with your ex.

Showing emotion will only fuel your narcissistic ex's desire to exploit your vulnerabilities. Instead of getting caught up in their words, step back and observe from a distance, as this will help you to stay composed and in control. Remember, you have the power to choose your reaction.

You can choose whether or not you will rule your emotions or whether they will rule you. It is only natural that you will have feelings that, at times, can come and go like waves in the ocean. To manage your emotions effectively, reflect on your feelings and focus on becoming more self-aware.

Emotional management techniques (EMT) can help you cope with the emotions that inevitably arise during co-parenting. These techniques involve recognizing and regulating your emotional responses to different situations. It is vitally important for you to remain calm and level-headed when dealing with your ex to avoid provoking them further.

Finding healthy emotional management techniques that are personalized to suit your unique needs is essential. Keep in mind that what works for one person may not work for someone else since every one of us is so unique.

To discover what methods work best for you, set aside some time to explore different relaxation techniques like mindfulness meditation, expressive writing physical exercise, spending time with loved ones, or creative activities. This will help you find what brings you the most happiness, peace, and calmness.

Mastering your emotions will also set an excellent example for your kids and can create a more peaceful co-parenting environment that is far easier for you to manage. Getting a handle on your feelings can have a positive impact on your life because you will be able to:

- make more rational and thoughtful decisions.

- objectively analyze situations and respond appropriately.

- communicate more effectively.

- resolve conflicts with greater empathy and understanding.

- enjoy better emotional, physical, and mental well-being.

- maintain healthier interpersonal relationships and boundaries.

Boundaries

Leaving a narcissist takes courage; well done. Many women become trapped in a cycle of narcissistic abuse, which they never escape, and the impact can be detrimental to them and their kids. Sadly, many women choose to stay instead of taking action.

Some women accept their partners' behavior and live for the "happy" times when their narcissistic partners are not around to drain and emotionally manipulate them. You made a wise decision to leave your narcissistic ex. While you have lost a lot of time that you cannot get back and did not protect yourself as you should have, you came forward and put an end to a bad situation.

Narcissists often try to control the conversation or push their ideas and opinions without regard for anyone else's views. Therefore, setting boundaries can prevent your narcissistic ex from controlling the conversation and determining how and when communication will happen.

Establish and enforce clear boundaries when cutting emotional ties with your narcissistic ex. Healthy boundaries can include taking a conscious step back from:

- arguments, disagreements, and negative talk.

- personal attacks, expressing frustrations, and blame-shifting.

- back-and-forth or looping conversations.

- going down any rabbit holes with the narcissist.

- discussing the past and oversharing.

When you communicate with your ex, always keep as much communication as possible to email and SMS exchanges. If you pick up that your conversations with your ex are becoming hostile and emotional, call them out on their behavior. Be relentless and keep calling them out on unacceptable behavior until your ex removes all emotion from their communication.

Instead, focus your attention on the following:

- Keeping your kids' schedules and needs front of mind.

- Being open to compromise and fostering a positive co-parenting environment.

- Calling out the narcissist until all emotion has been removed from discussions.

- Paying attention to harmful patterns.

- Escalating disturbing behavior to email.

When communication is focused on the kids, everyone involved benefits. As such, actions should provide a sense of trust for the kids' sake, and anything negative that can affect them should be avoided.

The chances are good that your ex regularly prioritizes his own needs and desires above the well-being of your kids. Call him out on his behavior, and as a loving, responsible parent, prioritize your kid's physical, mental, and emotional well-being.

Your ex is your ex, and they do not need to know everything that is going on in your life. You should not share information about all personal aspects of your life. If you are unsure about what you should and should not share with your narcissistic ex, ask yourself if the issue in mind is linked to the kids.

It is important that you begin to let go of any unrealistic expectations that you may have of your narcissistic ex in relation to his role as a parent. The sad reality is that if he has never made any effort before, he will not necessarily make an effort now. Remember that your new life is separate from your ex, so, keep your distance and slowly squeeze him out of the areas where he no longer fits.

Mindful Decision Making

Your needs and clarity of mind matter; you know that, and your ex must know that too. Take your time when making decisions or responding if you need to.

Do not feel pressured to give instant answers and make spur-of-the-moment decisions. If you cannot figure out what kind of response you should give in a particular situation, take a breather, think about it, and then answer.

It's time for you to take your life back, and your ex does not have the right to drag you into a corner where you are forced to make quick decisions. Your ex must learn to respect that there could be times when you will need some time to make decisions.

Do not commit to things you do not feel comfortable with. You are fully entitled to have your needs and wants respected. The days of you being forced to lead a life where you agree to things under pressure are over. For clarity, take a blank piece of paper and write down the advantages and disadvantages of each choice. Weigh it up. Revert only after you have reflected and are satisfied that your decision is aligned with the life you want to create.

Stay authentic and be true to yourself. You spent so long living to please your ex, and now you are living to please yourself and your kids. Live your best life as authentically as you possibly can. Do not allow your ex to steal any more of your valuable time and energy.

Communication Tools

When you end a relationship with someone who you do not have kids with, it is far simpler because you do not necessarily need to talk to them again. Whereas having kids with your ex means you must communicate for their sake.

Naturally, when a relationship ends, inner scars need to heal, and this healing does not happen overnight. Soon after a breakup with your ex, the wounds are still open, making effective verbal communication almost impossible.

While your wounds are still fresh and raw, it is wise for you to keep all communication in writing until you have both worked through most of your negative emotions. Be mindful that as you heal over the years, it should be easier for more verbal communication.

Minimizing Verbal Exchanges

Modern technology gives us so many options when it comes to communication methods, so use this to your advantage. Do your very best to avoid telephone conversations with your ex.

While communicating over the telephone may be more convenient, you cannot keep a clear record of your communications. Also, things you say on the phone could easily be misunderstood or manipulated.

Emotional Detox Techniques

Cutting emotional ties takes time and effort but can lead to tremendous personal growth, self-awareness, and a fulfilling future for you and your kids. Essentially you will need to undergo an emotional detox from your narcissistic ex, and one way to do an emotional detox is by visualizing the cutting of ties.

Cutting Emotional Ties Visualization

Visualization is a type of mental imagery where you use your senses to create an experience in your mind. There is no right way to use mental imagery; many people do it differently. Yet it is imperative to note that some people cannot create mental visuals in their mind's eye at all. However, the more you practice, the easier it will become.

Cutting Cords

Our emotional and energetic ties are believed to interfere with our ability to move forward, achieve goals and live our best lives. The cutting of cords visualization is a simple yet effective practice that can help you to move forward to a more positive and fulfilling life in a powerful way.

Using cord-cutting techniques, you can cut ties at the root of the problem, like parental and ancestral lines. The great thing about cord-cutting practices is that you can even teach your kids techniques that will help them to deal with any anxiety and stress they may be struggling with.

Learning cord-cutting techniques can help eliminate emotional and energetic ties you may have with other people or situations, including your ex. Cutting cords through visualization involves imagining yourself physically severing ties with the narcissist and freeing yourself from their negative energy.

Attempting to cut cords with a narcissistic ex may seem overwhelmingly difficult, but you absolutely have to do it for your own emotional and mental well-being. By cutting these cords, you can release yourself and start moving forward with far greater confidence and clarity. Additionally, the cord-cutting technique is also a fantastic way for you to develop self-awareness and emotional intelligence.

How to cut cords:

- Find a safe, quiet, and peaceful place.

- Get into a comfortable position.

- Focus on relaxing your body and mind.

- Close your eyes.

- Focus on your breathing.

- Take a few deep breaths.

- Call in your higher self and any divine beings.

- Visualize a cord connecting you to the narcissist.

- Visualize cutting through this cord that connects you to your ex.

- As you cut the cord, feel a sense of relief and liberation.

- Mentally say: "I am tearing up all karmic contracts I ever had with this person. I have learned my lessons, and I am happy to move on."

- Imagine pulling the roots out from your energetic system and throwing them away.

- Mentally repeat affirmations like "I release you from my life" or "I release all negative energy associated with this situation."

Repeat this visualization for at least 21 days to ingrain it into your subconscious mind. Through cord-cutting, you can let go of negative emotions and energy that may be holding you back and instill a sense of closure and peace in your life. Envision yourself being cleansed of all and any toxic energy once attached to you.

Exploding of the Rose Visualization

Every person experiences feelings of hurt and exhaustion when a relationship ends. After being in a toxic relationship with a narcissist, the pain, negative emotions, and feelings of exhaustion are amplified. Take the time to practice techniques that will help you to process your emotions to move on healthily.

The exploding of the rose visualization technique helps with releasing your ex's energy and taking back your own.

Visualize a rose in front of you. See the rose in vivid detail, including its color, shape, and texture. Imagine any negative thoughts and emotions linked to your ex that you might be holding onto. See this energy flowing from you into the rose and filling it up completely.

Then imagine the other person and watch any of your negative energy stored in them flowing into the rose while seeing any positive, energetic parts of you held in the other person drifting back to you.

When the rose is full, visualize it exploding in a burst of light and color. See the energy of the rose dissolving into the universe, leaving you feeling lighter and more peaceful.

When you attempt this visualization technique, as a rule of thumb, fill any energy gaps with positive, uplifting energy that you want to bring into your life. Imagine an extremely bright white light surrounding you, supplying you with sparkling, new energy.

Imagine a caring, helpful, and supportive circle of family, friends, and divine beings who will support you during this difficult time. By focusing on the positive energy and your support network, you will begin to release and return any negativity you have been holding onto.

Visualizing giving back your ex's energy and taking back your energy can be a powerful tool for healing and moving on. By focusing on the positive, you will soon start to feel better and move forward with new confidence and the strength you need to thrive in the future.

Meditation for a Healthy Mindset

Our minds can often become cluttered with thoughts, worries, and distractions that prevent us from thoroughly enjoying the present moment. This clutter can make thinking in a healthy way difficult.

In recent years, meditation has become extremely popular and can be used to slow down your mind and create space in your busy life and between your thoughts. Using meditation, you can calm your mind and better manage negative emotions, anxiety, and stress. Meditation can help you to cultivate greater awareness and inner peace.

Meditation involves sitting quietly while focusing on your breath or a particular affirmation to help bring your focus back to the present moment. Simply by focusing on your breath, you can quieten inner chatter, create space between your thoughts, and become more grounded and centered.

The benefits of regular meditation are well-documented and include the following:

- boosted immunity

- improved mood

- increased creativity

- increased self-awareness

- lowered stress levels

- mental clarity

- a greater sense of overall well-being

Divorce Coaches and Support Groups

When emotions run high, making sound decisions can be challenging. A divorce coach acts as a neutral third party to provide a steady hand, help you heal, and help you make informed decisions.

One of a divorce coach's main goals will be to help you establish boundaries with your ex. They can help you understand a narcissist's tactics and guide you on how to respond appropriately.

Divorce coaches can provide you with strategies to remain calm in the face of narcissistic behavior, which can help protect your mental health. They can also help you navigate divorce's complex legal and financial aspects.

Divorce support groups can also be precious resources to help with healing after your separation. Support groups can offer a safe place to share your stories, frustrations, and progress. You can connect with people with similar experiences and learn healthy coping mechanisms and strategies.

Support groups usually have professionals who provide both guidance and support, and sessions are confidential, giving you the freedom to express yourself without fear of judgment. A support group can help you move beyond the pain and trauma caused by the narcissist to find healing and peace. You will be taught the importance of self-care and self-compassion and learn to take responsibility for your recovery.

Mental health professionals can guide you in developing a healthy and constructive approach to managing your emotions effectively. Support groups tailored for people like you who have similar life experiences can be an excellent option to help you process your experiences and emotions.

Cutting Financial Ties

A narcissist will use two crucial weapons against you; your kids and money. Granted, cutting financial ties with a narcissist can be extremely tough, but it can and must be done. Cutting financial ties may include closing any joint banking accounts and selling joint assets. This will also help reduce stress and offer you both the opportunity to start afresh.

When you cut financial ties, it will also give you both a sense of finality and remove any financial co-dependency that may have been present in your relationship. This sends a message that you really mean business. Remember that it would be very unwise of you to leave any unfinished business, as loose ends can unexpectedly come back to haunt you.

Below is an example of what can happen when we leave loose ends with a narcissistic ex.

After Maria proved in court that her narcissistic ex was abusive to her and the kids, she got full custody. Maria then found a new apartment, and she and the kids moved out of the family home. Maria's partner continued to live in the family home after agreeing to pay the full mortgage.

At the time, Maria did not have the strength for another battle and did not insist that her ex move out of the family home so that they could settle things once and for all. This, however, blocked Maria's mortgage application for a house she wanted to buy because she was still financially tied to the old mortgage. Two long years later, Maria's ex has still no intention of moving out of the family home, and Maria has no way of getting finance for a new home.

In the next chapter, we will look at bringing more clarity into the co-parenting conversation.

Chapter 2:

Bring Clarity Back to the

Conversation

No one saves us but ourselves. No one can, and no one may. We ourselves must walk the path. –Buddha

Embrace, own, and honor your unique life journey with self-reliance and self-empowerment. While many people wish that someone would magically appear and rescue us from unpleasant situations, this will not happen.

You alone are responsible for your well-being and happiness, and you alone can take steps toward achieving your goals and creating a fulfilling life. One of the things that make fulfillment in life possible is good communication.

The trouble is that people have such unique personalities and experiences that we cannot always communicate with everyone similarly, especially not narcissists. That said, despite what you think, you and your narcissistic ex will and can communicate in a healthier way.

Once you and your ex can communicate effectively and have prioritized your kids, you are on the right path. The path you will be on will lead you to a place where you can raise healthy, well-rounded kids with bright futures ahead.

In this chapter, we will take a deeper look at communicating with clarity so that when you communicate with your ex, your messages are understood, and conflicts are resolved in a healthy way.

It's Over; What Now?

Brace yourself because when communicating with a narcissist, not everything is always as it seems. Communicating and co-parenting with your narcissistic ex will require you to remain calm, open-minded, and level-headed.

Written communication can be a valuable tool to bring clarity to situations that arise concerning your kids. When you focus on bringing transparency back to your conversations with your ex, a whole new world of possibilities opens up. Once you prioritize clear communication with your ex, you will find that you become far less frustrated and may even communicate with more compassion and understanding.

Decide to move forward with a new sense of confidence and control. Instead of continuously falling for the narcissists' toxic communication tactics, take control. Taking control may be something you need to learn to do, but after all that you have been through, you know the importance of taking the lead and especially, the consequences of not taking the lead.

Once you have learned how to take control of situations and emotionally disengage, you can begin to set higher standards for yourself and your ex. Few people realize this, but the reality is that once you raise the bar, the narcissist will mimic your behavior.

Healthy communication requires effort from both parties, but you can lead the way. You can reach mutually satisfying resolutions by approaching conversations with an open, clear mind.

Just as you would like to be heard, actively listen to your ex's thoughts and opinions and acknowledge their perspective. By doing this, you can create a more productive dialogue and a positive and collaborative exchange of ideas.

When it comes to building a new healthier co-parenting relationship with your ex, start small. The Great Pyramid of Giza was not built in one day and naturally would have required some form of management. Taking control of your relationship will make it possible for you and your narcissistic ex to take things to a whole new level.

Despite your ex's selfish tendencies, once you are in control, there are ways to communicate effectively. You can start to take control and build your confidence levels so that you can enjoy more effective and transparent communication with your ex by:

- Using a powerful affirmation like, "I choose to speak with clarity, and my messages are understood."

- Remaining calm and maintaining a calm demeanor when communicating.

- Using clear, simple, and precise language.

- Being direct.

- Practicing active listening.

When a person with narcissistic personality disorder feels as though their ego is being threatened in any way, they can quickly become aggressive or even defensive. By remaining composed and level-headed, you can play an essential role in preventing unnecessary arguments and outbursts and keep the conversation constructive.

Using simple language is not because you think your ex is stupid. You are doing it so there is no room for words to be twisted. Remember that, a narcissist can and will use any ammunition you give them.

Effective Communication Tools

Wouldn't it be wonderful if conflict between you and your ex ceased? While disputes are inevitable, they are also manageable with the right approach.

To empower yourself for effective communication and healthy living, repeat these affirmations often until they are engraved within you:

- I choose my way.

- I am brave.

- I am strong.

People with NPD thrive on drama and conflict. Consciously anticipate, and step back to find ways to resolve and handle issues as they arise.

A distorted view of reality and a lack of empathy makes communicating with a narcissist difficult, to say the least. It is hard to communicate effectively with someone who believes they are always right and will manipulate conversations and make themselves out to be the victim. Let your attitude and actions speak louder than words; your ex will soon start to disengage from emotional exchanges.

BIFF Technique

Conflicts arise every day, everywhere, and are inevitable. Most conflicts in everyday life occur due to misunderstandings and differences of opinion, and the priority is to resolve these peacefully. Using the BIFF Technique, you can resolve personal and professional conflicts, including those with your narcissistic ex.

When dealing with your ex, remember that they crave attention and drama. The more you feed that craving, the more likely it is that a narcissist will continue trying to get a reaction from you. Using the BIFF technique can help to reduce the amount of drama by removing any emotional triggers. The goal is to communicate effectively while minimizing the potential for arguments or misunderstandings.

The BIFF technique can also help you communicate effectively with your narcissistic ex without escalating difficult situations. Let's look at the BIFF Technique:

- Brief

- Informative

- Friendly

- Firm

Brief

The first step to BIFF is to keep your message short and relevant. The more you ramble, the more likely your ex will find something to twist or use against you. Avoid beating around the bush when you are dealing with a narcissist.

Be brief but polite, as being polite to others does not cost us anything. At the same time, ensure your communication is not so warm that your ex sees a gap to control or manipulate you. Do not allow yourself to be diverted.

Concise communication is essential when you sense that the topic may trigger intense emotions. Clear and concise language lets you get to the heart of issues and avoid unnecessary arguments. By keeping it brief, you can avoid dwelling on negative points and focus on healthy resolutions instead.

Keep all communication precise and formal, always stick to the point and the facts, and use short, clear sentences. Always remember to keep the lines of communication open and flowing for your kids' sake. Choosing to communicate only when necessary means that you are not only protecting your well-being but that of your kids.

Informative

When communicating with your ex, ensure your message is informative by providing facts without adding emotional commentary. Be clear. Say what you need to say, and express your thoughts in a way your ex can easily understand.

Address all your concerns accurately and objectively. When you are informative, you can convey your thoughts accurately and objectively without confusing your ex in any way.

Friendly

Friendly communication creates a better environment for productive discussions. A kind, calm, friendly, but professional tone of voice will keep the conversation peaceful and help avoid misunderstandings with your ex. Being respectful will help avoid unnecessary confrontations and make finding common ground easier. Your ex will see that you appreciate their opinions, even when they differ from yours.

Firm

When communicating with your ex, maintain firm boundaries and expectations. Being assertive and decisive with your words helps to display confidence and can help you avoid being labeled indecisive.

Being firm does not mean being rude or aggressive toward your ex; it means standing by your position without belittling your ex's opinion and finding solutions. Being firm in your communication shows confidence and assertiveness that can lead to practical win-win solutions.

The BIFF technique does not guarantee peace and harmony, but it can be useful when communicating with your narcissistic ex. Keep your messages brief, informative, friendly, and firm, and avoid engaging in emotional exchanges. Maintaining your boundaries and expectations is essential as well as focusing on finding ways to coexist and co-parent without unnecessary conflict or drama.

Active Listening

A narcissist seldom listens to what others have to say. As a result, to have a productive conversation with a narcissist, you must focus on actively listening to your ex's views. This may involve paraphrasing and clarifying what your ex is saying, ensuring you understand their perspective.

Listening to people who have different views can be challenging. This aspect of communication demands that you and your ex consider each other's viewpoints, accept what is reasonable, and disregard what is not.

While your ex has NPD, there may very well be instances where their perspective is correct.

Power of "I"

Dealing with a narcissist means that you are familiar with misunderstandings. The good news is that communication with your narcissistic ex can be improved when you use "I" language.

Using "I" statements can help you to take accountability for your emotions without your ex feeling as though they are being attacked. When using "you" statements, your narcissistic ex may become defensive, leading to failed conversations and conflict. To avoid this, use "I" statements and shift the focus toward yourself.

By intentionally using "I" language, you can significantly reduce conflicts and avoid triggering your ex's defensive reactions. "I language" focuses on expressing your emotions and needs rather than blaming another person.

For example, instead of saying to your ex, "You never ever listen to me," you could rather say, "I really feel so frustrated when I feel that I am not heard." This approach can help your ex feel less attacked and more open to feedback.

Using "I" language can help you to assert your boundaries without appearing aggressive or angry if your ex feels that their ego is threatened. When you speak from a personal perspective rather than "*attacking*" the narcissist directly, you can express your needs without triggering your narcissistic ex's defensive mechanisms.

Narcissists often interpret criticism or feedback as a personal attack and may respond with hostility or defensiveness. Using "I" language can help build trust and mutual respect so that you and your ex both feel heard and understood.

Power of Writing

Keep as much of your communication with your ex as humanly possible in writing. Choosing writing as a preferred form of communication can lead to more effective communication between you and your narcissistic ex. Additionally, writing can allow you to convey more complex messages easily.

Soon after a romantic relationship ends, both parties are emotional. Remember that you are entitled to choose communication methods you are comfortable with and that work best for you.

Written communication is a strong ally as it allows you to communicate without emotion or manipulation. It also gives you a conversation record, preventing misinformation or false claims. When communication is in writing, it gives you security and backup if ever needed, and it is more difficult for someone to deny having said something.

Use SMS for regular exchanges and emails when issues need to be "escalated." Your ex will soon know that when an SMS exchange is reformulated in an email, that exchange has escalated. Always keep your emails short and to the point. This will leave little room for misinterpretation.

A great thing about emails is that they can easily be kept, printed, and filed. While you may be a person who absolutely hates paperwork and filing, email correspondence with your ex is worth that extra effort. Filed correspondence between you and your ex can also help you keep track of any repeated negative patterns; if needed, you can forward them to your lawyer.

Another added bonus of written communication is that it allows you time to think over communication before you reply to it. Communicating in writing will enable you to step in and out of discussions and reflect before answering. Also, when you use writing in this way, you can even ignore your ex if they are trying to love bomb or suck you back in.

Maintaining boundaries can be challenging when you communicate face-to-face or on the telephone. There is phenomenal power in the spoken word, and a commanding energy exchange happens during verbal communication that does not necessarily occur when communicating in writing.

Parenting Plan

Another helpful communication tool is learning how to set a manageable co-parenting plan. Co-parents may find short-term goals far more accessible and more productive than long-term goals by providing a more realistic and measurable objective.

The chances are good that your ex may attempt to block or sabotage these goals, so work toward an objective your ex will not be able to obstruct. When co-parenting, propose workable goals for your kids' best interests.

Mediation

Sometimes, having a neutral third party present during difficult conversations is helpful, and mediation is something you and your ex may benefit from. Mediation allows for discussions in an environment that will allow for equal participation and a space free from any toxic dynamics that may cause tension.

Mediators can also help to facilitate discussions and clarify misunderstandings as they arise. Additionally, contacting a mental health professional can provide you with new and effective communication strategies. In the next chapter, we will have a closer look at the narcissist.

Chapter 3:

Understanding the Narcissist

A thousand enemies outside the house are better than one within -Celtic Proverb

While the exact causes of NPD remain unknown, many experts believe that several factors may be responsible, including:

- genetics

- early childhood experiences

- parenting styles

Narcissism can also develop due to overindulging or catering to a kid's every whim, which leads them to believe they are entitled to special treatment and attention. Sadly, certain traumatic life events may also contribute to people developing narcissistic traits. Whether it is nature or nurture, the end result harms the person with NPD and those around them.

While narcissists may seem charming and incredibly confident, they are deeply insecure. It is important to recognize the signs of narcissism and protect yourself and your kids from toxic behaviors. Family units are supposed to be our refuge from enemies and challenges. Unfortunately, life can become nearly impossible when a person in the family unit is a narcissist.

The narcissist is mostly focused on creating chaos, and this is what both follows and surrounds them. Life is tough with a narcissist, especially when they are provoking and doing their best to drain their closest and dearest to feed their insatiable self-serving needs.

Sadly, some narcissists get great satisfaction from seeing others suffer. A narcissist lacks empathy and struggles to understand the feelings and perspectives of others. When co-parenting with a narcissist, maintain firm boundaries and do not allow a narcissist to manipulate or control you. With understanding and caution, it is possible to protect yourself from the harmful behavior of a narcissist.

The Game of One-Upmanship

Affirmation: "I am grounded. I stay in my story."

When a narcissist is trapped in their fantasy world, nothing else really matters to them, and they are self-absorbed and unstable. Narcissists live in a bubble believing that everyone and everything should revolve around them. Preoccupied with fantasies of power, success, and admiration, the narcissist believes they are better than everyone else.

A narcissist's behavior can become a significant problem for them, eventually leading to social isolation. Narcissists tend to have a narrow circle of friends and family, who they often end up pushing away because of their narcissistic behavior. Narcissists can become so preoccupied with their fantasies that they do not realize how badly their toxic behaviors affect situations until it's too late. The chances are that your ex never realized how serious you were about leaving until you and the kids had left.

Constant game-playing can mentally drain and confuse any stable person. The reality is that the narcissist treated your relationship like a complex game of chess that was filled with draining mind games. Unfortunately, the narcissist believed that the more they treated you as though you were worthless and you accepted it, the more they could outsmart you. When you said "right," the narcissist said 'left.' If you said 'go,' then the narcissist would stay 'stop.'

Besides the constant mind games, you had to deal with control, deceit, envy, rivalry, and manipulation. And the absolute cherry on the cake is when the narcissist makes out that they are the victim in the situation and even attempts to use the kids against you.

By remaining grounded and rooted in your story, you can make better choices and avoid being swayed by the narcissist. Always ask yourself questions like: What do I want? Is this the best solution for me and the kids? Is it in our best interests? Is this going to limit me or help me grow?

What You Can Control

Affirmation: "I trust life, and I let go of what I cannot control."

Throughout your life, there are, have been, and still will be, many things that are beyond your control. The weather, other people's actions, and the natural progression of events are all things that are beyond your control. It is easy to become consumed by frustration or disappointment with the uncontrollable aspects of life, but remember, you can control your actions and thoughts.

Of course, focusing on what you can control is easier said than done. Getting frustrated over the things you can't change can be tempting, but this will only drain the energy that you have and distract you from your goals.

Narcissists are highly manipulative and incredibly frustrating to deal with, and you cannot control their behavior. While there's no easy solution for managing a narcissist, a helpful approach is to focus on the aspects you can control and let go of what you cannot. For example, you can set boundaries with the narcissist to minimize their negative impact on your life, but you can't control their behavior or personality.

By accepting the limitations of what you can manage and shifting your attention and focus to the things you can change, you can cultivate greater peace and productivity in your life. While it may take some practice, this mindset can help you to navigate the most challenging situations with extraordinary grace and ease. Focus on the end goal; raising well-rounded kids and having positive and peaceful relationships.

Handling the Narcissist

Ego

Affirmation: "I acknowledge and appreciate my efforts and those of others."

Do not fight or argue with your narcissistic ex, no matter how difficult it becomes, and always keep a cool head. Refuse to feed that craving for attention and admiration at all costs.

Simply put, a narcissist expects to always be the center of attention. Your narcissistic ex needs to be constantly validated and affirmed in not only their beliefs but their actions as well. Narcissists love attention; positive or negative; so keep it positive, or it will turn into trauma bonding as a form of control.

Show gratitude, compliment, and thank them when deserved: they will appreciate the compliments as they probably accused you of not complimenting them enough when you were together. The insatiable narc always complains of not getting enough attention when they are actually getting all the attention.

Empathy

Affirmation: I am kind and compassionate.

A narcissist lacks empathy and is unable to connect emotionally. You have lived in the face of emotional instability, provocation, confusion, and chaos. Practice being positive, generous, and accepting that there will be times when your narcissistic ex demonstrates their irrational side. Do not let your narcissistic ex's behavior rattle your cage; it's their problem, not yours.

Affirmation: "The Universe is watching over me. Help is at hand."

The narcissist has the twin characteristics of being overly concerned with their public image and being a coward. You have probably repeatedly seen how your ex takes no responsibility for their actions. Protect yourself by surrounding yourself with other parents, teachers, therapists, the police, and lawyers. There is power in numbers, so keep yourself covered. Make your ex aware that you are not alone on this journey and remind them often; eventually, they will get tired of trying to bait you.

Narcissists cannot afford to risk damaging their reputation as they may still be trying to rehabilitate their public image if you successfully exposed them in the past.

Power and Control

Affirmation: "I check in with myself before entertaining any demands."

Narcissists have a strong need for control and power. They manipulate and exploit others to achieve their goals and feel threatened when they are not in control. Let your ex know the world is watching them.

You have probably been doing this your entire relationship, which is checking in and out of the relationship by leaving the house. You probably spent more time outside than inside the home. The same principle of checking in and out applies here. Keep conversations in writing and check out of them when they take a turn that does not suit you. Take a step back. Let unproductive conversations go, or give a reply that aligns with your values in your own time.

Prepare yourself as the narcissist might still attempt to give orders, try to control, make things sound like an obligation, and try to be the expert on every topic. If they insist on making demands, they are welcome to do whatever they themselves demand of you.

Changing the Narrative

Affirmation: "I abide by my standards and values, and I seek the best."

Fret not; you can change the storyline by making your ex live up to your standards for a change. Soon your ex will realize that you will no longer accept their low standards or tolerate their dishonesty and that they will need to shape up. They will quickly realize you will no longer sit back while they control the narrative. The days are gone when you will tolerate them changing the subject and using intolerable distraction tactics.

Finally, you will take the steering wheel and gain control of your co-parenting relationship, formally considered a runaway nightmare. From now on, when your ex tries to pressure you into taking orders from them, you can stand tall and not be swayed.

Make your ex understand that you will no longer participate in heated emotional exchanges or in back-and-forth draining conversations that only upset you.

Lead by Example

Affirmation: "I focus on win-win situations."

Harness your ex's penchant for rivalry and envy to your child's advantage. One way to do this is to use it to motivate them to achieve your goals. Encouraging them to compete in healthy ways can drive your narcissistic ex to work harder and strive for success like never before.

Narcissists believe they are superior beings. To prove their superiority, everything is a competition, and they have to win. Use this characteristic to encourage the narcissist to compete with you in providing for the kids in the best possible way.

Remember to take photos of the kids doing activities on holidays and forward them on. Cook new dishes with the kids and take pictures of them. Do not hesitate to compliment the kids and show appreciation for the narcissist's effort. The narcissist will realize over time that they are, after all, good parents. This is wholesome soul food for your kids and a win-win-win situation for everyone.

Areas to avoid competing in:

- buying presents for the kids.
- giving your kids unhealthy foods.

- spoiling your kids.

- giving them a sense of entitlement.

Read how Angie led by example:

After separating, Angie was surprised to see a dramatic change in her ex's behavior. Now, Sam always seemed to obtain his holiday leave in line with the custody agreement. If Angie ever brought the kids on holidays, Sam would organize holidays for the kids too. Instead of repeating the old, negative behaviors of competing with Angie's strengths to undermine all of her efforts, Sam did everything in his power to be as good a parent, if not better than her. Likewise, lead by example and harness your ex's competitive streak to your advantage.

Negative to Positive

Affirmation: "I stay on high ground irrespective of the situation."

You have the potential to turn your narcissistic ex into a powerful positive role model and influencer for your kids. Keep your ex invested in the kids and show appreciation for this contribution.

Give your narcissistic ex positive roles in your kids' lives. For example, if your kids throw a tantrum or get upset, allow your ex to play a part in soothing the kids over the telephone. In this case, you will give your ex a different role from what he is used to. Usually, your ex thrives on upsetting the kids, but now you are giving him a role to do just the opposite.

Play your ex at his own game. When the narcissist feels like he is contributing positively to his kids" lives, he will work harder to continue doing so. The kids will also value this; it takes the pressure off you and reinforces your values.

As a loving, attentive mother, it could become quite upsetting if you notice that any of your kids are behaving like your narcissistic ex. If you see concerning behavior, take a deep breath, keep calm, and involve your ex. Below is an example of this situation and how best to handle it if it comes up:

Mary has 2 kids, a 9-year-old boy and a 6-year-old girl. Mary's son insults his little sister. Mary calls out the behavior without making references to the narcissistic ex. She then sends an SMS to the narcissist, describes the bad behavior, and asks her ex to discuss the issue with their kid and to stress the importance of not insulting others. The narcissist will then be expected to discuss the behavioral issue with the kid that he, himself, is guilty of. When your ex calls out his own kid for behavior that he is guilty of, he will be under pressure to set a better example in the future.

Gratitude, Recognition, and Validation

Affirmation: "I remember to say thank you."

The situation may seem tricky when it comes to showing appreciation to your narcissistic ex. After all, narcissists are known to be self-absorbed and often prioritize their needs over others. Fortunately, you can show gratitude to your narcissistic ex without enabling their negative behavior.

Firstly, acknowledge the actions or behaviors of your narcissistic ex that are worthy of thanks. This approach helps shift the focus away from the narcissist's negative traits and emphasizes their positive attributes.

Instead of focusing on the narcissists' ego, point out what they have done that has positively impacted others or helped the situation somehow. This will likely be more effective in getting your narcissistic ex to listen and appreciate your gratitude.

Next, setting boundaries when showing appreciation to your narcissist ex is crucial. This approach helps you not inflate the narcissist's ego to the point where they may start taking advantage of you. You can still express your appreciation by setting boundaries while protecting yourself from their toxic behavior. Maintaining clear communication and emphasizing mutual respect can go a long way in ensuring that boundaries are respected.

Below is an example of showing appreciation to a narcissistic ex:

Amanda noticed that after the kids were born, her husband Jim became less and less available, so much so that she began to perceive him as an absent partner and father. Since the custody battle, he had taken his fair share of responsibility, and Amanda could see a drastic increase in the quality of her life, both because she had time out from the narcissist's ongoing harassment and also from full-time caring for the kids. She now had more time to pursue her activities and interests and was very grateful for her ex's involvement in caring for the kids.

Affirmation: "I am grateful to my ex for his efforts."

Narcissists need to feel recognized and validated for their accomplishments, and they can become defensive or angry if they feel that their achievements are not being acknowledged or appreciated.

Show gratitude to your narcissistic ex for his efforts. Compliment the kids when the narcissist buys them new clothes or does fun activities with them. This will probably be a far cry from the days you were living together because back then, you did not have the headspace or the patience to thank him for anything.

To avoid any seething resentment down the line, keep the lines of communication open between your kids and their dad. Let your ex have his role as a father and be a stable, supportive mother.

Below is an example of keeping the lines of communication open:

Samantha found that when she heard her kids complain or accuse her of not seeing enough of their dad, she always put them on the phone to talk to him so they could plan to see each other. This way, the kids calmed down and stopped accusing her, and their dad felt validated. Another win-win-win situation.

Accountability

Affirmation: "I am attentive to what's happening around me."

With an inflated sense of self-importance, narcissists believe they are special and entitled to certain privileges. They also consider that rules that apply to everyone most certainly do not apply to them. When a narcissist is expected to follow the same rules as everyone else, they may become angry or resentful.

Behind the external façade of superiority imposed on others, narcissists have no real plan for their lives or desire to evolve in any way. A narcissist's lack of drive is precisely why you can set the tone and maintain standards.

As a responsible parent, you can set the bar higher for your sanity and your kids' well-being. A narcissist will often disregard the opinions and needs of others because they think others are undeserving of their attention. Narcissists have a grandiose sense of their abilities and exaggerate their achievements. They are also prone to extremes by exaggerating their accomplishments and ignoring their mistakes.

Because of this, stay on top of all issues when dealing with your ex by doing the following:

- Let nothing fester.

- Formalize everything.

- Stay as informed as possible.

- Discuss and document issues.

Be mindful to keep the professionals in the loop of any issues when necessary. Stay alert to avoid any type of manipulation from your narcissistic ex, and be attentive to what's going on.

Parenting Styles

Narcissistic parents tend to be intensely critical, controlling, demanding, and sometimes even neglectful of their kids' emotional needs. When kids don't get the love and affection they need, they can feel neglected and insecure.

Unfortunately, growing up with a narcissistic parent can make kids feel like they are not good enough, and they might even resent their parents. Sadly, many kids raised by narcissists often struggle with low self-esteem and battle trusting others or forming meaningful relationships.

One of the most damaging parenting styles seen with narcissists is authoritarian parenting. The authoritative style is based on the idea that a parent is never wrong, and the kid's opinions do not matter. Narcissistic parents who adopt this style tend to set unrealistic expectations, causing their kids to feel overwhelmed and stressed.

The permissive parenting style is another style often seen in narcissists. This parenting style involves a lack of boundaries and consequences, leading to impulsive and entitled kids. Narcissistic parents who adopt this style may materially spoil their kids but not give kids the emotional support they need.

Certain parenting styles can cause serious harm to your kids' development and well-being, and kids raised by narcissistic parents may suffer from anxiety and depression.

Embracing different parenting styles and being flexible with your ex is key to creating a workable co-parenting situation. When dealing with your narcissistic ex, accept that you may be unable to change their behavior. Brace yourself because you will need to be as flexible and adaptable as possible regarding parenting styles, especially with a narcissist.

For example, when your narcissistic ex uses harsh and aggressive discipline tactics on your kids, try addressing the situation non-confrontationally. You can try talking to your narcissistic ex about more positive forms of discipline, like time-outs or taking away privileges. Alternatively, you can embrace their disciplinary style and find a reasonable compromise that works best for everyone.

Never let your feelings toward the narcissistic parent get in the way of what is best for your kids. Encourage positive behavior from your ex when you can and show your kids that it is possible to work with difficult people.

Embracing different parenting styles with the narcissist does not mean giving in to their demands or tolerating abuse; it simply means finding a healthy way to co-parent.

When to Engage, When to Be Kind, When to Withdraw

Suppose that your ex is being abusive toward either you or your kids; document the behavior and take action. It may be helpful for you to keep an email thread of all the issues you have with your ex by topic. Remember to formalize and document all matters pertaining to their inappropriate behavior.

Watch out for toxic patterns, be vigilant, and do not hesitate to call professionals if you need to. Know when to engage, when to be kind, but most of all, when to withdraw.

Listen to and trust your intuition because this powerful tool can help you navigate life. When something sounds off, take the time to stand back to understand why it seems off and then ask yourself the right questions. Taking a step back and checking in before responding to people and situations can give you an entirely different perspective.

Here is an example of a problem that Alice had to handle with her ex concerning their daughter:

Alice's kids told her in great detail that their dad had insulted their daughter by calling her a degrading, inappropriate name unfitting for any woman or girl, especially not a girl of 8. The kids explained how guilty their dad felt afterward.

Alice later spoke to her ex about the incident and was met with an instant denial. Her ex persisted in trying to distract her and move to other topics and attempted to avoid taking responsibility by expressing his shock at the accusation.

Alice held her ground, re-stated why they were speaking, gave her take on the issue, and closed the conversation. She noted the incident in a separate email. Alice already had a thread of emails detailing other inappropriate conversations her ex had had involving their children. Alice closely monitored the issue and was prepared to contact her lawyer if necessary.

Be ready to contact your lawyer if necessary, but choose your battles wisely. Once custody of the kids has been determined, keep court battles to a minimum.

Avoid shifting any drama, which was—after all—the nature of your relationship, to the courtroom. Do not risk becoming locked in old, negative energies that are very time-consuming and will take you away from focusing on yourself, your kids, and moving forward in life.

Be mindful of where and how you use your energy. You want to avoid creating unnecessary expenses or giving your power away to lawyers.

Chapter 4:

It's All About the Kids

To be in your children's memories tomorrow, you have to be in their lives today -
Buddha

Life is an incredible adventure filled with so many beautiful things for you to appreciate, learn and enjoy. Parenting is most definitely one of the most amazing and rewarding experiences you will have in life.

When your kids come into this world, your life changes quickly. Everything you do from thereon is and will always be with their best interests at heart. As a parent, your most important job is to lay a solid foundation for your kids so that they can navigate life confidently. Your role as a parent is to do everything in your power to ensure your kids develop into self-sufficient, independent people who thrive in life.

While many parents wish they did, kids do not come with individual instruction manuals. There are countless parenting books available to new parents, which can cause confusion, especially when these books often give contradictory advice.

Kids are the most extraordinary gifts you can have in life and also your greatest responsibilities, and you want to ensure your kids always feel safe, secure, and loved from birth. Parenting is about far more than meeting your kids' immediate physical needs but their emotional ones too.

As a parent, you want a solid, life-long relationship with your kids based on respect, love, and compassion. Act with compassion, kindness, and self-awareness when raising your kids. Doing this creates an environment where they can grow and develop into well-balanced, happy people.

Home

Home should be a place filled with unconditional acceptance, love, kindness, encouragement, and deep connection. Give your kids the priceless gift of freedom, and never stop working on creating an honest and trusting relationship with them.

Always treat your kids with love and kindness. Your kids are innocent and pure beings who should not face and should be protected from any form of trauma. Remember that it is crucial for you as a parent to always practice what you want to preach. Be a parent who leads by example and teaches your kids how to navigate life by displaying positive, empowering behavior that is aligned with your values.

Raise your kids in a nurturing environment that encourages emotional intelligence, curiosity, and creativity. Work on creating a positive, fun space for your kids within the home. Provide your kids with inspiration, friendship, and learning opportunities that will nurture their natural abilities.

Encourage your kids to question life and the world without fear of failure or judgment. By doing this, your kids become more aware of their individuality and abilities, which will help them blossom in all areas of their lives.

Structure and Routine

Our everyday actions and habits are important and contribute to our overall quality of life. We often build circuits inside of us for habitual actions that run in a very deterministic fashion.

When we perform a particular activity, our brain releases a chemical called dopamine that signals that the action is pleasurable. As a result, we will likely repeat the same actions to attain this pleasant experience. This creates a loop of cue, routine, and reward, which overrides our conscious decision-making faculty, ultimately leading to habitual behavior.

Be consistent with your kids' routines and structure, as this can set the tone for a calm environment. A chaos-free environment with routine and structure can help your kids form healthier lifestyle habits.

Good habits and discipline go hand in hand and form the basis for success in life. Discipline is essential in achieving a balanced and productive life and does not need to be motivated by fear or punishment. Encourage kids to:

- develop healthy habits that contribute to a balanced life.

- eat healthy food.

- get enough sleep.

- maintain a routine that focuses on their physical, mental, and emotional well-being.

- spend time on positive, creative, or productive activities.

As a parent, you can also guide your kids into forming the habit of being kind to others. When your kids are kind to others, this can help them to:

- feel like they belong.

- form meaningful connections that are associated with happiness.

- grow into compassionate and considerate adults.

- have a more empathetic approach to other people.

- have improved self-esteem.

Encourage your kids to give compliments and share their toys, food, and belongings with others. This will help instill a sense of generosity and selflessness in them from an early age.

Positive Memories

Honestly, 21 years go by quickly, and you always want to be as involved in your kids' lives as possible. The truth is that your kids are born, and then before you realize it, they are adults and ready to take on the big wide world.

Every day is a precious gift in which you can focus on having fun moments and creating joyous memories with your kids. The reality is that when you actively focus and work on raising kids with fun and positivity, this will benefit not only your kids but you as well.

Focus on bonding with your kids through conversations, laughing with them, singing together, playing musical instruments or listening to music, telling stories, and watching television together.

As a committed, loving parent, plug into your kids' lives as much as possible. Immerse yourself in your kids' school and other activities. Your kids will understand that you are incredibly proud of them no matter what and that they are your first priority.

Creating a Positive Home Environment

Creating a positive, fun space for kids at home is important for helping them learn, grow, and thrive. Safety, creativity, and comfort are important factors to consider when you create a home environment for your kids to explore and be creative.

Make sure that your kids have different art supplies, crafts, games, and space. Delve into your kids' interests, like music, painting, or drawing, and guide them and always support and encourage them to learn new things.

Encourage your kids' interests or talents. Whenever your kids show an interest in a particular activity, give them the necessary tools and materials to help them explore their interests further. Whatever you do, avoid forcing your kids to do activities they are not interested in.

Depending on how old your kids are, you could consider creating a little dress-up corner with various costumes and make-up they can experiment with and use to bring their imaginations to life. Think of creating a dedicated art station, study, or music corner. If your kids are younger, you could even have an area where they can play "school." When you creatively incorporate different play elements into the home, you encourage your kids to use their imagination and be creative.

Just like you need a quiet, tranquil, and welcoming space, so do your kids. Create a calm area that supports concentration and learning, specially designed to help your kids focus on reading, creative writing, or any other quiet activity they prefer. Make sure that this space is inviting and a place where they want to spend their time.

Make your home as cozy and comfortable as you possibly can, as this allows your kids to feel relaxed and secure in their space. Think creatively and add items like soft pillows, blankets, rugs, or even bean bags so your kids can feel snug and comfortable while performing everyday activities.

Ensure that your kids' rooms are well-lit and get enough air to help them maintain focus and avoid uncomfortable temperatures. Soft background music or nature sounds at a low volume can also create a relaxing environment for you and your kids to unwind in.

If your living environment allows it, try to ensure your kids can access some outdoor space, whether it be a backyard or a balcony. Spending time outdoors and exploring nature can greatly benefit their overall well-being.

With plants, play equipment, and furniture, you can create a healthy, safe, educational, and fun environment where kids can engage in outdoor play. By focusing on elements of comfort, play, and outdoor exploration, you can encourage your kids to explore the outside world and grow.

Creating a home where your kids can be authentic is your responsibility as a parent. Kids need a space that they are proud of to call their home. Encourage your kids to invite their friends over to your home. When you open your home up to your kids' friends, this gives you the opportunity to get to know your kids' friends better.

With some imagination, creating an engaging, comfortable, positive, fun, and welcoming space at home that your kids will love, can be easy and inexpensive. Consider working together with your kids to personalize the area and let their creativity shine while celebrating their unique interests.

Create A Win-Win-Win Situation

During the legal proceedings, Kate asked her lawyer to mention the kid's activities in her court submission. This was firstly to ensure that the costs of the activities were shared between both parents, but also, documenting the activities officially made them harder to ignore.

The kids were involved in competitive sports, and their presence was strongly recommended every week; otherwise, overall team performance was impacted. When Jonathan did not bring the kids to their activities on several occasions, Kate suggested collecting the kids from school and bringing them on the days she did not have custody of them. Johnathan then picked the kids up directly after their activities. Kate also gave permission to their older son to leave school alone and go to his swimming class at the swimming pool next to his school. This way, the kids were not deprived of their activities because of the separation. This was a win-win-win situation.

Bonding and Building

Always be emotionally in tune with your kids. Love them, listen to them, validate them, and always be responsive to them. Encourage your kids to identify their emotions and name the feelings that they are feeling. Kids must learn to express their feelings with words instead of acting out on them. Remember, your kids must be able to express themselves and their emotions authentically.

While things may be difficult with your ex, always keep a 'united front' in front of the kids and keep your kids out of adult battles. Do not overshare or overwhelm your kids with adult emotions, as this can put the kids in an awkward position and could force them to pick sides. Always talk about their dad positively.

Avoid statements that will cause your kids to stress, like:

- You are just like your father.

- Your father has no respect for the rules I put in place.

Resilience

Resilience is developed from two aspects of brain functioning. Conditioning: is how you encode events in your brain, and neuroplasticity: is the mechanism that allows the brain to grow and rewire through new experiences. New experiences can create positive or negative changes in the brain.

Parenting is also about building resilience in kids and teaching them that they can bounce back from difficult experiences with a positive mindset. The aim is to rewire old dysfunctional patterns of behavior and build new neural circuitry by:

1. Remaining calm in the face of a crisis.

2. Developing clarity to see your internal reactions to an experience as well as see the experience for what it is.

3. Connecting with loving, supportive people.

4. Using your abilities to enable quick and effective action.

5. Drawing on courage to always persevere.

Remember that when kids feel safe and grow up in an environment without abuse and low family stress, they are more likely to develop resilience. Additionally, your mental health as a parent and your parenting style can affect whether your kid will be resilient.

Encourage your kids and let them know you appreciate them. Be consistently warm and attentive yet firm and not overindulgent. Remind your kids often of their freedom of thought and speech.

Teach your kids how to put up their emotional insulation when your ex becomes irrational. It is vitally important that your kids feel empowered enough to set healthy boundaries. Kids need to know what is and what is not appropriate behavior.

Address critical issues like:

- boundaries that your kids need to have if your ex speaks negatively about you.

- dressing themselves.

- respecting their bodies.

- sleeping in their own beds at night.

The Universe Is Watching Over Me, Help Is at Hand

Kids need to learn how to maintain a positive mindset and build resilience despite any challenges they may face. Powerful affirmations can instill a strong mental foundation that can help support your kids throughout their lives. In a world where we may have to overcome negative feedback and opinions, affirmations can go a long way in instilling a greater sense of self-worth and self-assurance in kids.

It has been proven that positive affirmations can reduce anxiety levels in kids and improve their mental well-being, creating a lifelong foundation of growth mindset and self-confidence. As a parent, you can teach your kids practices which can help them overcome challenges and overwhelming emotions.

Using affirmations, kids can approach challenges positively, knowing they have the courage and capability to face any situation boldly. When kids use affirmations, they feel empowered to believe in themselves and their abilities.

Teach your kids to celebrate and recognize their uniqueness makes them stand out and shine. Affirmations can encourage kids to appreciate their individuality and can show them that being different is okay.

Kids need to become aware of the power of affirmations and positive thinking from a young age. As a form of positive reinforcement and encouragement, kids can recite affirmations before bedtime, in the morning, and even throughout the day.

You can help your kids create unique affirmations by engaging them in the process, using age-appropriate language, and pointing out their personal achievements and progress. A few examples you can teach your kids include powerful affirmations like:

- I always do my best.

- I am a good person.

- I am calm and peaceful.

- I am capable of achieving my dreams.

- I am courageous and capable of facing any challenges.

- I am loved and valued.

- I am unique and special.

- I am worthy of respect and kindness.

- I attract good things.

- I can achieve all that I set my mind to.

- I can think for myself.

- I have the right to express myself.

- I'm going to take time out and read a book.

- Maybe I'm not perfect, nobody is, but I love myself.

- My feelings are important and matter.

Be mindful that positive thinking facilitates learning and enhances your kids' academic performance, communication skills, and emotional intelligence. When your kid feels down, encourage them to repeat affirmations like "I am capable" or "I am loved." With practice, this will help your child to build confidence and self-worth.

Positive self-talk and gratitude are essential and powerful tools for developing emotional intelligence in kids. One way to encourage your kids is by noting what makes them happy - however small. Find out your kid's interests by asking them to share one thing that they are grateful for during bedtime routines or dinner.

Encourage your kids to openly communicate and share their feelings with you and be compassionate to their thoughts and feelings. Do this by speaking openly and honestly with them about their emotions. As they age, role-play difficult conversations, or ask your kids to think of solutions to their problems.

Storytelling can also be used to encourage gratitude. Stories can be powerful tools that you can use to communicate emotionally charged lessons with your kids. These stories can be real-life stories or simply sharing experiences that your kids had during their busy days. By having conversations about gratitude and self-talk, you will begin to help your kids form positive relationships with themselves.

Teach

When you keep criticizing your kids, they don't stop loving you. They stop loving themselves. –Buddha

As a parent, you are tasked with modeling healthy behaviors and teaching your kids how to navigate life successfully. Sadly, many parents leave teaching kids up to schoolteachers, where parents should be their kids' primary teachers. Focus on being a compassionate parent who prioritizes gentleness and caring over criticism and reproach.

Encourage, educate, and inspire your kids to always do their very best while setting an good example of what a decent human being really is. Some essential things that you can teach your kids include:

- basic household chores

- decision-making

- treating others respectfully

- working with money and time

- personal health and hygiene

- problem-solving

- relationship building

- self-improvement techniques

- personality disorders

Narcissistic Personality Disorder (NPD)

Help your kids understand the importance of showing understanding and compassion to all people from different walks of life. Also, teach your kids about NPD, its effects, and how to deal with anyone with this personality disorder. Encourage your kids to reflect and put themselves in someone with NPD's shoes. Your kids must understand that people with NPD should not be negatively judged.

Teach your kids to recognize manipulative behavior in people. Explain to your kids that if anyone tries to make them feel guilty or uses flattery or false compliments to get what they want, these behaviors are signs of NPD.

Explain to your kids that NPD can cause people to behave in complex ways. Help your kids realize that NPD affects how a person perceives and thinks about the world.

Your kids must understand that they may notice their father acting self-centered, demanding, or as if they are more important than others. Encourage your kids to be understanding and compassionate while focusing on building a healthy relationship with their father, even under challenging circumstances.

Problem-Solving

Kids who are seen and heard are more confident individuals. Acknowledge the positive things that you notice about your kids. Be a role model by modeling resilience for your kids, instilling respect, and fostering critical thinking skills. Avoid power struggles at all costs and foster responsibility. Teach your kids how to identify and take ownership of problems and always have reasonable expectations of your kids.

Identifying problems, generating solutions, taking action, and discussing how well your kids worked builds self-confidence. When kids recognize their actions, their self-esteem grows, and they start believing they can contribute positively.

With critical thinking skills, life is easier. Sadly, kids who do not have the necessary critical thinking skills tend to avoid issues when they arise. Teaching your kids critical thinking skills is a vital part of emotional intelligence. Remember that depending on your kids' age, your approach to teaching critical thinking may vary; however, you can start teaching these skills by doing things like:

- brainstorming potential solutions to problems with your kids, explaining the consequences of each, and encouraging logical decision-making. You can also facilitate complex problem-solving by helping break down problems into manageable parts and encouraging creative thinking and compromise.

- setting goals for your kids regarding critical thinking and problem-solving. Always start with small goals and build them up as your kids achieve them.

- modeling problem-solving by tackling problems maturely and logically. Often, kids repeat what they see at home, so if you are a great role model for your child, you are paving a great pathway for their success.

- identifying ownership of problems is crucial for personal growth, and you can encourage your kids to think about who is responsible for their problems. As a responsible parent, teach your kids to identify and face difficulties. By taking ownership of problems, kids become more responsible and proactive in addressing issues they might face. Teaching kids how to own their problems also helps them become more accountable, confident, and independent.

- educating your kids with reading or watching materials that challenge them to think outside the box. Talk enthusiastically about all the pros and cons of different decisions, possible alternative outcomes, and different points of view. Creatively use role-playing and act out scenarios with your kids where they must actively find solutions. This can help your kids understand the dynamics of problems, so they get used to dealing with them. You can also role-play with your kids and teach them how to leverage each other's strengths when tackling complex problems.

- playing games and inspiring creativity. Play board games, puzzles, and other activities that require your kids to think outside the box. Also, let your kids create their own games to encourage them to become inventive and creative.

- explaining the importance of problem-solving and trying to give examples of solutions to real-world problems. Framing can be a collaborative effort to help your kids understand how working together can lead to creative solutions.

- motivating your kids. Remember that you should be your kids' biggest cheerleader, so celebrate their skills and successes. Always recognize and acknowledge your kids' successes and encourage them to think about how they solved problems. Encourage your kids to ask questions and look for answers during daily activities.

- remembering to zip it. Allow your kids to problem-solve. Give your kids time to think of solutions or answers instead of you giving answers.

Behavior and Discipline

From the time your kids' brains started developing within your womb, essential changes occurred as they grew. Our prefrontal cortex is responsible for regulating our actions, emotions, and thoughts and is only fully developed at 25.

Be empathetic to the changes that your kids are going through during adolescence. Your role as a conscious parent is to be a logical presence and guiding light. Bear in mind that your kids' bad behavior can be a cry for attention, and to always show warmth and love.

Stay on top of any behavioral issues with the kids and be aware that kids from abusive homes may start to replicate their parents' behavior. The kids themselves will often even replay the dynamics of the parents amongst themselves.

Exposure to any form of abuse can profoundly impact kids. Research shows that kids raised in abusive homes will likely become abusers themselves (World Health Organization, 2022). Become a role model your kids can be proud of and teach them healthy relationship behaviors.

Be assertive and observe your kids' behavior toward each other, you, and your ex. Behaviors to pay special attention to include:

- manipulation

- dishonesty

- lack of cooperation

- sense of entitlement

- lack of respect

- insulting attitude

- inflated ego

- low self-esteem

Call your kids out and document any negative behavioral patterns you pick up on. If you pick up that your kids are being dishonest, you are going to need to address this in a positive way. Honesty is one of the most beautiful and valuable qualities anyone can possess, and it is essential for successful relationships, personal development, and growth.

Encourage your kids to be truthful and sincere in everything they do, as honesty is the foundation of trust and respect. You can instill honesty in your kids in various ways, like:

- setting a good example.

- correcting them with kindness when caught lying.

- encouraging them to take responsibility for their actions, even if it means owning up to their mistakes.

If you struggle to discipline your kids, do not hesitate to get therapy, or help from teachers and the community.

Disciplinary Strategies

When it comes to discipline, consistency is key. One useful disciplinary strategy is redirection which can be powerful in keeping your kids on track. This seemingly simple tactic involves distracting your kids from misbehavior and pointing them toward more positive and productive activities.

Polite Requests

Using polite requests is another disciplinary strategy that can be helpful for you and your kids. Teach your kids to be respectful and considerate by using gentle reminders instead of harsh commands. This approach helps establish healthy communication between you and your kids and can lead to positive behavioral changes without punishment or tears.

Time Out and Time In

Time out and time in is another effective discipline strategy when used correctly. Time out gives kids a chance to take a break from a stressful situation and an opportunity for you to reassess challenging events. Time out and time in involves actively engaging with your kids during stressful or misbehaving moments and providing them with support and guidance through those tough times.

Mutual Problem-Solving

Mutual problem-solving and seeing challenges as opportunities is another essential part of disciplining your kids. Encouraging your kids to work with you to identify and solve problems fosters a sense of teamwork and cooperation that can benefit you and your kids. Plus, it teaches kids essential conflict resolution tools they can carry throughout life.

Consistency

Consequences for misbehavior must always be consistent and must not be overly harsh. Approach disciplinary situations with your kids with patience and understanding, as every child is unique, and their reactions may differ. Take the time to tailor corrective strategies to fit your kids' personalities and behavioral patterns.

Love Languages

Your kids' bad behavior can also be a desperate cry for attention. Always show your kids warmth and love. The five love languages include:

- words of affirmation

- quality time

- physical touch

- gifts

- acts of service

From showing physical touch through hugs and kisses to providing words of affirmation and quality time spent together; love languages offer a framework for ensuring that you are meeting your kids' unique emotional needs.

Decoding your kid's preferred love language early on can foster positive behavior. So, whether it's gift-giving or acts of service that make your kids light up like a firework display, take the time to learn how to speak their love language fluently—it could be a game-changer.

Parental Alienation

Be alert, watch for any signs of parental alienation, and quickly nip it in the bud. Parental alienation can significantly impact your kids' mental and emotional health. In situations where kids feel as though they must choose between their parents, they can feel guilty, anxious, or even depressed.

Parental alienation is a serious issue during a separation or divorce, especially when one parent is a narcissist. The dangerous aspect about parental alienation is that, in your case, it will involve your ex manipulating your kid's emotions.

When kids are outright denied contact with one of their parents without a legitimate reason, this can also be a form of parental alienation. This could happen if your ex manipulates the kids into not wanting to be with you or communicate with you.

As a narcissist, your ex is a master manipulator, and the chances are good that he will try to manipulate your kids at some point. It's essential to keep your eyes and ears open and watch out for signs of parental alienation like:

- kids suddenly becoming hostile toward you.

- kids suddenly not wanting to spend time with you.

- kids suddenly saying negative things about you.

If you notice signs of parental alienation, speak to your kids and do not hesitate to act. Listen to what your kids say about how their dad treats them, and document everything—what he asks them to do and his opinions of you.

Parental alienation can affect your kids' future relationships, especially if they believe healthy relationships can be manipulated or controlled. Remember that early intervention can help prevent long-term damage to your kids. Once you have spoken to your kids, handling the situation effectively will mean:

- sending your ex an email about what the kids have told you.

- setting clear boundaries within that email regarding his manipulation tactics.

- making it clear that his behavior is not acceptable and needs to stop.

- documenting everything.

- seeking a lawyer or mediator to help you manage the situation if needed.

In the next chapter, we will explore what conscious parenting looks like so that you can be the parent your kids need and deserve.

Chapter 5:

Conscious Parenting 101

The most precious inheritance that parents can give their children is their own happiness. –Buddha

As a parent, you are your kids' haven and a soft place to fall. Most older people were raised by parents who were disciplinarians and did precisely what they were told to do when they were told to do it, no questions asked. Sadly, even today, some parents do not realize their kids are unique and can teach them a few things.

The truth is that a parent's ego is not there to stunt the growth of their kids in any way. Kids need to be free to develop into their true selves. Creating a safe, loving environment where your kids feel secure enough to express themselves freely is a priority.

Caring for You

Dealing with your narcissistic ex can be extremely challenging, especially regarding conscious parenting. Narcissists are known for being self-centered and lacking empathy toward others, including their children. However, by practicing these techniques, you can help mitigate the adverse effects that your ex's behavior may have on your children. This means openly and honestly communicating with your kids about their emotions and validating them.

It also involves setting clear boundaries with your ex and consistently enforcing them. Additionally, it is important to prioritize self-care as a parent to maintain your emotional well-being and model healthy behaviors for your kids. While looking after your kids' needs, it is also important to look after yourself.

After surviving narcissistic abuse, practicing self-care is absolutely crucial to the healing process. Remember, healing takes time, and it's okay to take things slowly, be patient, and focus on doing whatever helps you feel your best. Self-care activities can include things like:

- getting regular exercise.

- getting enough sleep.

- eating a healthy diet.

- participating in therapy or support groups.

- prioritizing activities that make you feel good about yourself.

- setting healthy boundaries.

- learning how to recognize toxic personalities.

- avoiding toxic relationships.

While dealing with a narcissistic ex may not be easy, practicing conscious parenting can ultimately lead to positive outcomes for you and your kids.

Thriving Kids

Conscious parenting requires dedication and effort, but watching your kids grow and flourish with confidence, empathy, and self-awareness is incredibly rewarding. The practice of conscious parenting involves being fully present and mindful of your kids. It's about tuning into your kids' needs and emotions and responding to them lovingly and constructively.

By practicing conscious parenting, you can create an environment that fosters emotional intelligence, resilience and ultimately helps your child thrive. This means:

- being honest but compassionate about mistakes or difficulties.

- listening to your kids without passing judgment.

- modeling conflict resolution skills.

- modeling healthy communication.

- putting the well-being of your kids first.

- setting clear boundaries.

Conscious parenting means you must ensure that your kids live a life with consistency, discipline, and structure. A home with structure and routine sets the tone for a calm, less chaotic atmosphere where kids can thrive and develop healthier habits.

Mindfulness Techniques for Conscious Parenting

Parenting can be rewarding but also overwhelming and stressful. Practicing mindfulness techniques can help parents stay present in the moment and manage their emotions and reactions to better respond to their children's needs.

Some simple mindfulness practices that you can include in your daily life include things like:

- Being fully present when playing or talking with your child.

- Focusing on self-care through exercise or meditation.

- Paying attention to your thoughts and feelings.

- Practicing gratitude for all the positives in your life.

- Taking deep breaths during stressful situations.

By incorporating these practices into daily life, parents can become more aware of how their words and actions affect their children and can create a more positive relationship with their kids that is based on understanding and healthy communication.

Conscious parenting in action involves breathing, reflecting, setting boundaries, and accepting. One of the important aspects of conscious parenting is that parents look inward and focus on areas where they can improve and grow rather than focusing on their kid's behavior. Parents need to consider how they express themselves and their expectations. Conscious parenting requires you as a parent to look at the bigger picture.

I'm Not Perfect; Nobody Is

Abuse, in any form, leaves its mark on a person. You need to acknowledge that, like no one else is perfect, neither are you. Narcissistic abuse is something that you lived with for several years. The reality is that the chances are good that narcissistic abuse has impacted your mental health.

Always be mindful of and keep a check on your behavior. Sometimes, as humans, we can become so focused on the narratives we tell ourselves and our ex's flaws that we neglect to reflect on our flaws. Choose to manifest your potential, and do not dwell in the past.

Conscious parenting starts with developing a strong and positive bond with your child. As a conscious parent, focus on managing your emotions, thoughts, and behaviors when dealing with challenges. Be fully aware and in control of your feelings and limit negative reactions to your kid's behavior. Avoid getting angry, upset, or frustrated as much as possible, and practice calmness in the face of difficulties. Remember that your kid will adopt habits and characteristics they see in you.

Conscious Parenting Tips

Being a conscious parent means being aware of your actions and how your actions affect your child. Become a more mindful parent by listening to your kids. Take some time to consider if, when you are talking to your kids, are you really listening? If you notice that there have been instances where you do not always plug into what your kids are saying, please do not be too hard on yourself.

Active listening means focusing entirely on your kids when they are talking and trying to understand their perspective. When you start actively listening to your kids, this will help strengthen your connection with them and give them a safe space to express themselves freely.

Another vital part of conscious parenting is prioritizing self-care for you and your kids. Many parents often do not realize how important it is for them to care for themselves. How will kids know how to look after their emotional and mental health if their parents do not show them? Kids need their parents to model healthy behaviors.

Encourage your kids to engage in self-care activities like reading, exercising, or practicing relaxation techniques. By modeling this behavior, you empower your kids to improve their self-esteem and look after themselves.

Strive to give your kids positive reinforcement and avoid using negative language or harsh punishments. Using positive reinforcement to encourage desired behaviors can strengthen your kid's self-esteem and create a more positive relationship between you.

By avoiding negative language and punishing behaviors, you can teach your kids to make better and healthier choices and take responsibility for their actions. Becoming a conscious parent takes effort and practice but can positively impact you and your kid.

Identifying Dysfunctional Patterns

Becoming familiar with the dysfunctional patterns within you and your family is beneficial, but it should all start with you. It does not help to take the moral high ground and blame everything under the sun without reflecting on your behavior.

Take some time to consider the possibility that your behavior may traumatize your kids. Perhaps you have been so traumatized by narcissistic abuse that you are overreacting.

Keeping a journal will make monitoring behavior and picking up on dysfunctional patterns far easier. Here is a very simple way for you to begin honestly identifying dysfunctional patterns:

1. Start by noting down your behavior with your kids.

2. Create two columns.

3. Column One: What do you want to teach them, and what are you teaching them?

4. Column Two: Is there room for improvement?

Doing inner healing work is not for the light-hearted and will mean asking yourself some difficult questions that you need to answer honestly. If you lie to yourself, you are not helping yourself, and you most certainly are not helping your kids.

Consider asking yourself some difficult questions like:

- Do you speak with an all-knowing superior tone to your kids?

- Do you put your kids down?

- Do you humiliate your kids in front of others?

- Do you frighten your kids?

- Do you criticize your kids?

- Do you threaten your kids?

- Do you insult your kids?

- Do you shout at your kids?

- Do you pinch your kids?

- Do you push your kids?

- Do you make your kids cry?

- Are you too intolerant of your kids?

You can always try this exercise to monitor your behavior patterns and find out if you are misbehaving:

- Record yourself talking to your kids.

- Take note of your kid's responses to your behavior.

- Identify your triggers and take ownership of your responses.

- Analyze the behavior that you have recorded every night.

This exercise will help you identify the angry, nasty, corrupt, bitter, and vengeful part of yourself that you need to release. By going inward and releasing what no longer serves you, you can make room for healthier, more wholesome habits that you will put in place.

Note down all the statements you made to the kids. Then read them as if they belonged to someone else. Ask yourself the following questions:

- How many times did you insult or criticize them?

- How often did you lose your patience?

- Did you raise your voice to them?

This simple exercise ensures that you make ten times more positive than negative statements over time. Keep score of your behavior and aim for better every day.

Once you become more aware of and familiar with your triggers, establish a routine where you immediately incorporate self-soothing strategies. Self-soothing strategies could include things like:

- leaving the room.

- making a phone call.

- calling their father and putting the kids on the phone with him.

After thinking long and hard about your responses and having identified some of your dysfunctional behavior, consider consulting a therapist to help you work through things you need help with.

In similar ways that you have started evaluating your own behavior, you can use similar techniques to monitor your kid's behavior. Conscious parenting is also not just about making your kids happy at any cost. Your goal should be to raise well-rounded adults equipped to handle life's challenges.

When monitoring your kid's overall behavior, exclude basic house rules like brushing their teeth, showering, or bathing, and making their bed. Start by noting any serious issues you notice about your kid's behavior. Pay attention to patterns of behavior that persist over time, especially those that disrupt family life or social relationships. Observe your kid's behavior when they experience stress or disappointment. Ask yourself the following questions:

- Do your kids lash out or withdraw?

- Do your kids blame others quickly or take responsibility for their actions?

Let your kids know that their best interests are your main priority and that you can help them find professional support if they have issues, they feel they need help with. Move forward, focusing on reinforcing positive behaviors and building resilience through praise, positive reinforcement, and consistent routines. Every child's journey is unique, so tailor your approach to their needs.

Trying to practice conscious parenting with your narcissistic ex can be a grueling and challenging experience. You will likely have to navigate your ex's self-centered behavior constant demands for attention, and manipulative tactics in an effort to put your kids' needs first. It's essential to set clear boundaries and communicate directly with your ex while remaining calm and composed in the face of their emotional outbursts or attempts to trigger you.

Your kids' well-being should always take precedence over any conflicts or power struggles with your narcissistic ex. Stay committed to providing a safe, loving environment for them no matter what challenges come your way. The next chapter will examine how you can move forward and create a happier, healthier, and stronger new you.

Chapter 6:

The Healing Journey

The mind is everything. What you think you become. –Buddha

Our minds are powerful machines that affect how we perceive the world. When you realize just how important your thought life is, you will discover how your thoughts impact and shape your reality.

Be bold and connect with your authentic self and start working toward developing a new you. The time has come for you to begin moving beyond the overwhelming feelings that have dominated your life for so long and embark on an exciting journey of reinventing yourself. Brace yourself; you are about to focus on your needs and goals like never before.

Managing Your Mindset

At times in our lives, especially when you are going through difficult situations, it can be easier to shut yourself away from the world. No matter what, do not isolate yourself from the people that care for you. Huge benefits come with surrounding yourself with positive and supportive people.

Your kids need you to be the healthiest version of yourself that you can be. By choosing to surround yourself with positive and supportive people, you will rebuild your self-confidence, improve your self-esteem, and create a new sense of identity.

There are many instances where people become so trapped by the scars from their past relationships that they find it very hard to release the deep inner pain and resentment. Part of moving on includes practicing gratitude, acceptance, and forgiveness.

When you practice gratitude, you consciously focus on all the fantastic things in your life instead of the negative. Positive thinking is a proven method that can help you to release negative attachments and emotions.

For example, if a person has hurt you, it may be incredibly challenging to move forward and release the pain that you may feel. Changing your focus from your pain to the great things you have in life, such as friends, family, or a career, can help you move forward.

So many people do not realize that holding onto negative emotions and attachments only limits their potential. Practicing gratitude has an incredible way of helping you put overwhelming things in perspective. Often, people focus way too much on the things they do not have rather than what they do. Practicing gratitude helps you realize you already have much to be thankful for.

Acknowledging your life and relationship experiences, being bold enough to learn from them, and moving on is crucial. It's important to feel grateful for the good times you had in your relationship and to make peace with the fact that your once-cherished relationship is over.

Focusing On You

Healing journeys are profoundly personal but know that you are never alone. Many people are going through or have gone through exactly what you are going through right now. Stay focused on yourself while you are on your healing journey. While you may feel intense inner pain now, you will overcome this and become stronger and wiser than ever.

Choosing to reshape your entire life will propel you to a whole new level. You are courageous, as not many people can objectively introspect, identify, and make a conscious decision to be better and do better in life. It is amazingly encouraging that you realize the power to change your life lies in your own hands.

Living with a narcissist emotionally drains you and leaves you feeling and sometimes believing the lie that you are not good enough. Now you need to take time to refocus on yourself. While catering to your ex's whims, you have neglected your needs for way too long.

When you begin to value and refocus on yourself, you can find healthier ways to cope with your emotions. The reality is that while you were so busy with mundane tasks and responsibilities, you neglected your needs. Unfortunately, the needs we neglect often profoundly affect our emotional and mental health.

Moving forward toward a new you includes grieving and working through tough emotions. It is only natural to mourn the loss of a relationship after investing so much time and energy into it. Do not be too hard on yourself and allow yourself the time you need to grieve the loss of your relationship. But, while you mourn this loss, do not let your grief or depression consume you.

When you leave an abusive relationship, it is natural that you will want to move on with your life in a healthy way. You may be feeling totally overwhelmed and unsure of how you will get your act together, but rest assured, you have this.

Getting Your Act Together

Be proud of choosing to move forward and not stagnate. Take a deep breath and celebrate the fact that you have selected growth in your life. Your mind may be filled with racing thoughts, and you might have no idea where to start or how to pick up the pieces of your life.

You deserve to celebrate yourself for taking ownership of where you are in life and for not allowing the trauma to hold you back from all the wonderful things life offers. A few things that can help you to pick up the pieces of your life include:

- listening to and acknowledging your needs.

- prioritizing your emotional, mental, and physical well-being.

- setting healthy boundaries.

Take time to focus on your positive attributes and accomplishments. Recognize what makes you unique and write those things down.

Reflect on your characteristics often so that they become a part of your self-image. The more you focus on who you are, the more you can take control of your life and make good decisions.

Promise yourself that never again will you waste valuable time and energy trying to rationalize with narcissists or leave room for them in your life. Remember to stop and withdraw and draw a line in the sand regarding doublespeak and psychological game-playing. Know your worth and celebrate who you are. Remember that you are a fantastic person worthy of love and respect.

You deserve to be able to choose who stays in your life and who does not. Choose people in your life who treat you with kindness and understanding. Respect yourself enough to acknowledge and accept that you are entitled to look after yourself. Acknowledge that you are ready to do whatever you need to do so that you can live your best life.

Processing Emotions

When you are on your healing journey, self-compassion and self-care are essential. Unprocessed trauma can cause people to see life through a fearful, anxious lens and can result in them spending days and nights feeling tense and hypervigilant.

Make peace with the fact that you were an object in the narcissist's game that they call life. As you try to process the sea of emotions raging inside you, you need to accept some hard facts, including:

- Narcissists are not emotionally stable.

- Narcissists are self-absorbed in their fantasy world.

- You are not to blame for a narcissist's toxic behavior.

It is only normal that you are angry and even resentful. Anger and resentment are genuine and potentially destructive emotions that you need to find a way to process. If you allow anger and resentment to fester inside you, these negative emotions will affect your overall well-being.

For different reasons, many people stay in relationships with narcissists. The narcissist's continual boundary-pushing and toxic behavior takes its toll over time. Some people do not realize it, but being subjected to narcissistic abuse affects the hippocampus in the brain.

Long-term narcissistic abuse can trigger the release of stress hormones that can cause damage to the brain's neural pathways. Due to narcissistic abuse, the way the brain processes information changes, making it difficult for a person to make decisions and think clearly.

We end up forming a non-response to negative behaviors. Usually, when things go wrong, we have a fight or flight response; however, after being subjected to narcissistic abuse, many people end up going into a freeze stage. In this stage, we feel helpless and stay in the toxic relationship and take each day as it comes without responding to the negative behavior of a narcissist.

The effects of narcissistic abuse can be far-reaching and include other problems like:

- anxiety

- chronic post-traumatic stress disorder

- cognitive decline

- depression

- destructive behaviors

- hypervigilance

- inability to form lasting relationships

- inability to trust

- mood swings

- chronic pain conditions

- racing thoughts

- self-esteem issues

- self-isolation

- sleep disorders

- tendency to people please

Neuroplasticity

After living with a narcissist, it is not uncommon for people to become emotionally deregulated. The great news is that the human brain is capable of incredible things, and by working on rewiring the neural pathways in your brain, you can heal from the damage caused by narcissistic abuse and become more emotionally regulated.

Neural pathways are the connections between the neurons in our brains responsible for transmitting messages. When you repeatedly engage in a particular activity, the neural pathways in your brain associated with that specific activity strengthen.

Various techniques can help you become more aware of your thought patterns and emotions and understand the triggers that lead to negative thoughts and feelings. By gaining this awareness, you can change your thought processes and develop constructive and healthy thinking patterns.

Rewiring your neural pathways can restore psychological well-being but requires patience, self-reflection, and a willingness to learn new techniques and therapies. It is important to note that rewiring the neural pathways in your brain is usually an ongoing process that requires consistent effort and engagement. Be encouraged that with time, you will learn how to identify negative thought patterns and replace them with positive, healthy thought processes.

Different approaches that can be used to rewire our brains include:

- walking in nature

- art therapy

- learning new languages and skills

- learning to play musical instruments

- mindfulness practices

- participating in new sports challenges

- exercise

- reading

- traveling

Let us look deeper into a few ways for us to get rid of limiting negative emotions before they start eating you alive from the inside out.

Mindfulness Practices

Various mindfulness techniques, like affirmations, journaling, breathing exercises, and meditation, can help us to process negative emotions after narcissistic abuse. Mindfulness techniques help you to focus on the present moment, which can help you to reduce anger and improve mental clarity.

Affirmations

Powerful affirmations can be amazing healing tools when you are on your healing journey. One affirmation you can use is "I tune into myself." Remember, you really do owe it to yourself and your kids to do so. Be sure to ask yourself what you need and want in your life. Also, acknowledge the areas in your life that you could improve in.

Another powerful affirmation is, "Where my attention goes, my energy flows." You only have so much energy, and you need to use it wisely. Realizing where your attention goes is where your energy will flow to is one of the most positive things you can do for yourself. Take some time to do a personal energy audit to identify areas where you are giving too much energy.

The first affirmation that can help you to move forward from narcissistic abuse is, "I am worthy." Having experienced narcissistic abuse, you may begin to feel unworthy or undeserving of love, respect, and happiness. This affirmation can help shift your focus onto your worthiness and remind you that despite what the narcissist may have said or done, you deserve true love and happiness.

The second affirmation that can help you move forward is, "I am in control of my own life." A narcissist thrives on being in control and often leaves their targets feeling powerless. This affirmation can help you to fully understand that you have the power to make your own choices and that you are in control of your own life. Regaining control and acknowledging that no one else should have power over your life can be empowering.

Another empowering affirmation that can help you move forward is, "I release the past and embrace the future." After experiencing narcissistic abuse, you may find yourself dwelling on the past and replaying negative memories. This affirmation can help you release the past and shift your focus to creating a better future. It can be incredibly freeing to let go of negative memories and focus on looking forward to a brighter future full of possibilities and positivity.

Other powerful affirmations include statements like:

- I widen my perspectives.

- I move my life up a gear.

- I am complete as I am.

- I love myself; I am my own best friend; I champion myself.

- I live my best life.

Journaling

Another powerful tool to help you process your emotions, boost your self-esteem, and heal from narcissistic abuse is journaling. There is tremendous power when you put pen to paper and write down your feelings, expectations, and life experiences.

Journaling requires honesty and authenticity and means expressing your emotions and thoughts without judgment. Remember that by truly reflecting on and communicating your experiences and emotions, you can begin to heal and move toward healthier relationships and a more positive self-image.

Through journaling, you can:

- Identify your strengths and qualities.

- Gain insight into your actions and feelings.

- Identify negative beliefs or thought patterns.

- Understand how narcissistic abuse affected you.

- Process your emotions and experiences.

When you are trying to process your emotions, you can start by noting down any feelings and thoughts of anger that you may have as they arise. Pay special attention to things like:

- Did anything in particular trigger those angry thoughts?

- Was your anger directed at a specific person?

- Was your anger directed at a specific thing?

- What were you doing when you became angry?

- How did your anger manifest itself, perhaps in an image or a thought or both?

Once you have an inventory of the anger you are feeling, consider asking yourself the following questions:

- Is reducing your anger a psychological adjustment or a decision you must make?

- Is there something you can say or do that will reduce your anger?

Additionally, you can use automatic writing to get issues off your mind and onto paper, which has huge therapeutic benefits. This is also an opportunity to obtain some new and sometimes surprising perspectives.

Mantras

Believe it or not, people have used mantras for thousands of years as pathways to higher consciousness. Despite what many believe, a mantra is much more than a simple affirmation. The word mantra originally comes from the Sanskrit words "MAN" and "TRA." "Man" means a person's mind and emotional reality, and "Tra" means instrument, tool, or vehicle. So, in its entirety, the word mantra means instrument, tool, or vehicle of the mind.

A mantra is a sound or vibration that you can use to transport your mind from a state of busyness to one of stillness and deep meditation. Just by chanting mantras, we can protect ourselves.

Mantras can be used to help people return to their source: The universal energy that permeates all things. One such mantra that is commonly used for this purpose is "AUM," which represents the sound of creation and is widely believed to be the fundamental vibration of the universe. When chanted regularly with intention, this powerful mantra can help you really connect with your inner being, clear your mind of distractions, and tap into the universal consciousness.

The first step in using the AUM mantra to return to the source is finding a quiet, peaceful space where you can really focus without distractions. Calm your mind and body by sitting comfortably and then taking a few deep breaths.

From there, the mantra can be repeated either silently or out loud, focusing on the sound and vibration of each syllable. As the mantra is repeated, you should become fully absorbed in the sound and energy of the AUM, letting go of any thoughts or distractions that arise.

As you continue to use the AUM mantra to return to the source, it is essential to remember that this takes time and practice. Returning to the source cannot be achieved overnight but through a lifelong journey of self-discovery and spiritual growth.

By regularly chanting the AUM mantra, you can learn exactly how to tap into the energy of the universe and its infinite wisdom. Using mantras, you can discover new insights and perspectives to help you navigate life more easily and clearly.

Empowering mantras can comfort you, reassure you and help you recognize your undeniable strength and resilience. Mantras can help you believe in yourself again and realize you can overcome all challenges. Be encouraged, as using mantras allows you to replace your negative emotions and thoughts with positive ones.

Some examples of mantras you can use to help you heal from narcissistic abuse include:

- I matter.

- I am powerful and can overcome any obstacle.

- I am worthy of love, kindness, and respect.

- I am strong and capable of healing.

- I release all negative energy and replace it with positivity.

- I understand the meaning of real love.

- The opinions of others do not determine my worth.

- I am safe and strong.

- I love myself even if others do not.

- I accept myself and all of my strengths and weaknesses.

- I am worthy of the best in life.

- I love and honor myself.

- My first priority is my well-being.

- The joy of life is what matters.

Meditation

Regular meditation is another essential part of self-care that can help you process and release difficult emotions. By reducing stress, increasing self-awareness, and building resilience, meditation can help you heal from narcissistic abuse. Meditation can also help you recognize negative and anxious thought patterns, become aware of psychological triggers, and gain insight into the trauma that you have been through.

Here is an example of a meditation technique for healing from narcissistic abuse:

- Take a few deep breaths.

- Focus on your breath going in and out.

- Acknowledge your feelings and allow them to pass through your body. Sense where negative emotions are being stored in your body.

- Visualize your pain, hurt, anger, resentment, trauma, and all other negative emotions being released.

- Imagine a loving white light surrounding you that is healing and comforting you.

- Visualize this white light slowly entering and healing your body, soul, and spirit.

- See every cell in your body lighting up.

- Affirm that you are comfortable, safe, and secure.

- Repeat "I am the light, the light is all around me, the light passes through me, the light protects me, the light purifies me, the light heals me. I am the light, I am the light, I—am—the—light."

- Continue to visualize yourself surrounded by a loving light and healing yourself from within.

- Express gratitude for your inner healing.

- Remind yourself that you are healing and are taking your power back.

Be gentle with yourself; healing takes time. Be patient and compassionate with yourself and your progress. Regularly remind yourself that you do not need to suffer alone in silence and that you are surrounded by healing.

Visualizations

Self-esteem work and connecting with your inner child are possible using visualization techniques. Visualizations involve using imagery and creative techniques to create a sense of inner peace. They can help change negative thought patterns and internal dialogue. Using visualization techniques allows you to manifest your ideal life while balancing your energy.

Force of Light Visualization

One powerful visualization technique requires you to create a clear image in your mind and visualize yourself in a positive and empowered environment. To begin, you will need to take several deep breaths and focus on bringing your attention inward.

Visualize a special place unique to you, like a beach, a forest, or a mountain. Imagine that you are sitting or standing in that place and feel the elements around you. For example, the warmth of the sun, the scent of flowers, or the sounds of nature.

Take in the beauty and peacefulness of the scenery. Focusing on your breath and then drawing strength and resilience from this beautiful environment. Feel your trust and belief in yourself growing and blossoming like your surroundings.

Picture yourself being empowered and confident. Believe in your own strengths and gifts. Allow the feeling of great courage and self-assurance to flow through you, and imagine yourself as a powerful force of light.

As you are breathing in and out, affirm that you are strong and resilient. Let uplifting emotions take over, and imagine yourself growing in your power. Visualize the strength that now lies within you, driving away all other influences.

When you are ready, thank the environment around you for supporting and uplifting you. When you leave this place, you should feel refreshed and blessed.

Empowering Visualization

Another visualization technique you can use to help you move forward in life involves you closing your eyes and taking a few deep breaths. Next, allow yourself to relax completely and focus on the present moment. Now visualize that you are in a place that you find calm and peaceful. Try to create as much detail in your mind as you can, like colors, textures, and sounds.

Invite and welcome positive healing energy into your visualization. Imagine a white, healing light that fills your visualization with peace and comfort. Visualize any problematic people in your life as small, powerless figures. Imagine reducing their presence and size until they disappear entirely from your visualization.

Imagine yourself becoming bigger and brighter with every moment that passes. As you become bigger and brighter, you will feel more capable, powerful, and in control. Lastly, bring yourself back into the present moment. Bring the positive and empowered feelings that you experienced during your visualization with you as you open your eyes and refocus on the present moment.

Yoga

Any form of exercise can help you by releasing endorphins that will improve not only your mood but your overall well-being. Exercise is truly one of the healthiest ways to channel and process emotions into positive activity, which is important for long-term mental and emotional health.

The emotional instability caused by narcissistic abuse can oftentimes be debilitating. Manipulations, mind games, and trauma can leave you lacking self-confidence. Yoga is a spiritual practice that you can use to connect your mind, body, and soul.

Spiritual practices can truly help you cultivate a greater sense of self-awareness and mindfulness. Yoga can help you to rebuild your sense of self and power, heal from narcissistic abuse and let go of negativity that can be holding you back from achieving all that you can.

You can learn to retake control of your emotions with the help of yoga. Practicing yoga can also help significantly reduce things like anxiety, depression, and sleep issues which are often a direct result of narcissistic abuse.

Forgiveness

Because, in a sense, it's the coming back, the return, which gives meaning to the going forth. We really don't know where we've been until we've come back to where we were. Only where we were may not be as it was because of who we've become. Which is, after all, why we left. –Bernard, 'Northern Exposure'

Like many things in life, forgiveness is a choice and a profoundly personal matter which is entirely up to you. We can choose to forgive ourselves and others and move on or not, and the consequences of that choice can profoundly impact our lives. While forgiveness is a sticky subject for many, true freedom comes when you choose to forgive.

Life is an incredible journey, and each of us chooses our own lessons to learn during our time here. It is best to take full responsibility for our choices and actions, learn the soul lessons we came for and move on. When we look at forgiveness from a different perspective, forgiveness can become much easier.

The truth is that something incredible happens within you when you can hold yourself accountable, accept and forgive. When you accept and forgive, you leave little room for anger and resentment to fester.

Due to the lessons you have learned thus far, the next time a narcissist comes into your life, you will be more clued up to what's happening around you. You will be far less willing to believe your own false narratives or accept seemingly rational excuses for staying in a toxic situation.

When you forgive your ex and yourself, you can start to break the toxic cycle and create a peaceful life. Only once you have truly forgiven can real peace and acceptance take place.

When we consciously decide to let go of anger and resentment through personal accountability and forgiveness, we create a space for something positive to enter and change our lives. We are now on the verge of reshaping our lives and showing up as our best selves.

Own What Is Yours

Make an important pact with yourself that you will drop any co-dependent or enabling behavior by refusing to take on the roles and responsibilities of others. Let go of other people's burdens; they are not yours.

When it comes to your ex, it is no longer necessary to take responsibility for things that your ex should be responsible for. You are not the narcissist's mother, wife, or partner, and they are free to carry their own responsibilities.

When you are no longer taking ownership of responsibilities that are not yours to take care of, it forces the narcissist to stand up and take ownership. Once you are no longer carrying the roles and responsibilities of others, you will also find that you are far less stressed.

At all costs, avoid playing the blame game and, under no circumstances, label yourself a victim. You are not a victim but a powerful victor. Do not accept the narcissist's victim mentality and narrative either. When you can step away from the blaming and victim mentality, you create space for deeper understanding and compassion.

Self-Help Workbooks

Self-esteem and self-compassion workbooks provide holistic approaches to healing and embrace the idea of self-care so you can better realize your self-worth and tune into yourself more. These workbooks can give you guidance on how to work through difficult feelings and build self-esteem through different exercises and techniques.

In addition to providing practical tips and strategies for building self-esteem, these workbooks can also give you beneficial advice. Advice in self-esteem workbooks might include techniques on:

- positive self-talk

- realistic goal setting

- focusing on your unique strengths

While building resilience, anger, grief, and anxiety are all toxic emotions that you can work through with the help of self-compassion workbooks. With the help of self-esteem workbooks, you can go on an empowering adventure where you explore your own emotions, thoughts, and behaviors.

Empowering the Heart Chakra Meditation

Focus on your breathing. Feel your mind and body relaxing. Connect with your heart chakra and feel warm, loving energy. Feel this love expanding and expanding.

Visualize your favorite place on this earth—like a personal sanctuary. What emotions arise? Add this feeling to your heart chakra. Think of someone you love. Think about how you love everything about this person. Connect with these emotions and bring this emotion to your heart chakra.

Now think of an animal that you love or have loved. What are the emotions that you feel? Place these feelings in your heart chakra.

Remember a happy occasion. Perhaps a trip with friends or family. Remember how you felt. Was it happiness, joy, contentment, excitement? Feel all these emotions and blend them into a ball of positive, loving energy in your heart chakra. Imagine radiating this energy all over the earth and beyond.

Feel how you are glowing and allow all these energies to drop down to the earth. Set your intention to receive this loving energy back multiplied. Repeat to yourself, "I am receiving back multiplied what I am sending out." Thank the universe for these energies.

Support

Generally, people do not get married to get divorced. Divorce is an incredibly tough and emotional experience, especially when your ex is a narcissist. A healthy way of processing your emotions after narcissistic abuse is by seeking support.

Therapy

Our behaviors, feelings, and thoughts are all interconnected. Cognitive Behavioral Therapy (CBT) is a form of therapy that can hugely benefit you. CBT can help people change thought patterns into more positive, constructive, and realistic ones. With the help of CBT, you can learn new coping skills to better handle and overcome challenges, including Post Traumatic Stress Disorder (PTSD) and Complex Post Traumatic Stress Disorder (CPTSD). Using CBT, you can learn how to reframe the challenges you face.

Energy work can also help you to heal the internal wounds caused by narcissistic abuse. By working with trained energy practitioners, you can find a pathway to healing on a deeper level and improve your physical and emotional well-being.

Energy work involves using different techniques to balance and restore energy flow within your body. Narcissistic abuse compromises a victim's energy levels and leads to physical or emotional disturbances. Energy therapy can help release stuck energy and promote healing on a deeper level.

Reiki is another popular form of energy healing that uses the practitioner's hands to transfer energy to your chakras and promotes healing and relaxation. The goal of Reiki is to balance the energy centers in your body, which are known as chakras. Reiki has been shown to significantly reduce stress, improve sleep, and promote overall well-being.

Another popular form of energy work that can help you to heal from narcissistic abuse is acupuncture. Acupuncture is a form of traditional Chinese medicine practice that involves the placement of tiny needles into specific points on your body. The needles help to regulate the flow of energy, or Qi, throughout your body.

Studies have shown that acupuncture can reduce symptoms of depression, anxiety, and PTSD. By stimulating the body's natural healing processes, acupuncture can help you heal from narcissistic abuse to regain balance and peace in your life.

Another form of therapy that can help you whilst you are on your journey of healing after narcissistic abuse is Eye Movement Desensitization and Reprocessing (EMDR). EMDR therapy involves a trained therapist asking you to recount a specific past traumatic experience. At the same time, you move your eyes back and forth in a specific pattern. It is widely believed that EMDR can help your brain reprocess the traumatic memories and emotions that are associated with them, leading to a reduction in symptoms.

EMDR therapy is a relatively new but effective therapy for treating PTSD, CPTSD, and other psychological conditions. If EMDR therapy works for you, it can help you process the trauma so that you can move forward in a way that allows you to rebuild your self-esteem, regain control, and lead a happy and healthy life.

Emotional Freedom Techniques (EMT) or Tapping involves tapping specific points in the body to remove disruptive feelings trapped in the body. As you tap these specific points, you express the emotions you would like to externalize.

For a very long time, hypnotherapy has also been used to treat a range of conditions, including addictions, anxiety, and depression. In recent years, hypnotherapy has also been used to help people recover from the effects of narcissistic abuse.

During hypnotherapy, a relaxed state is usually achieved through guided meditation or visualization techniques. This relaxed state allows the therapist to access your subconscious mind to help identify and resolve underlying emotional or psychological issues. This process can help you to release negative emotions and beliefs and replace them with positive thoughts and feelings.

Magnet therapy is a non-invasive form of therapy that can help you to heal from the damage caused by narcissistic abuse. The goal of magnet therapy is to offer a natural way of promoting relaxation, reducing stress, and improving overall well-being. The concept of magnet therapy has been used since ancient times to aid in healing various ailments. It is believed that magnets have specific therapeutic effects on the human body.

Using magnetic fields has also shown promise in reducing pain and inflammation. It is believed that these magnetic fields stimulate the production of endorphins and reduce the production of stress hormones in your body. Magnet therapy can be beneficial in reducing the symptoms of narcissistic abuse, like anxiety, depression, and stress. There are various types of magnet therapy available, including magnetic jewelry, magnetic pads, and magnetic blankets.

Despite being a relatively new concept, magnet therapy has shown positive results for healing from narcissistic abuse. Using magnet therapy for narcissistic abuse should not be seen as the only treatment but rather as a complementary one to aid in the healing process.

Time Out

The importance of taking some time out for healing after being in a relationship with a narcissist cannot be stressed enough. Being in a relationship with a narcissist damages you on so many levels, and time is required to heal from the toxicity that you have been exposed to.

Man Diet

It is absolutely normal that after being in a relationship with a narcissist, you will feel invalidated and disrespected. The truth is that a narcissist does not really value their partner's emotions and emotional needs.

It is common for many women who have been in relationships with narcissistic partners to attract another narcissist. To avoid this happening to you, think about taking a step back from romantic relationships for a period of time. See it as a "*man diet.*" Yes, you heard me right, a *man diet.*

Sounds humorous, but by avoiding getting into a new relationship for a few months after your break-up, you decrease the chances of meeting another abusive person and ending up trapped in another toxic relationship. Let's face it there is absolutely no way that you want to end up in another toxic relationship after all that you have been through.

This thawing period will give you the time to work through any negative emotions that you may be carrying with you. Additionally, it will give you time to become more discerning about who and what you give your precious energy.

One of the worst possible things that you can do after being in a relationship with a narcissist is to rush into a new romantic relationship. By hurrying into a new relationship, you are not only putting yourself at risk but also your future partner. Not everyone is a narcissist, and you may be fortunate enough to meet a real gem, but you may end up hurting them because you have so many unhealed places within you.

By taking our time and observing people who come into our lives, we can learn a lot about them. Over time we often learn things about people that we never knew about when we first met them.

Take some time to write down all the qualities you would like to have in a potential partner, and then observe the people who come into your life. Observing repetitive gaps is an opportunity for inner healing, as those who enter our lives are our mirrors.

If you are dating, take it slowly and be authentic from the start, and test the relationship by affirming who you really are in that relationship.

Re-Inventing Yourself

Take some time to consider what the best version of you looks like. Have you got more money or a different career? Are you a happier or kinder person who is funnier and laughs more? Would you like to be more spontaneous and exciting, perhaps? Could you perhaps be a more attentive and loving mother and partner? Is the best version of you sportier and more fit? Once you have envisioned the person you would like to become and set milestones to make this happen, your energy will start to change, and you will begin attracting people who resonate with who you are becoming and not who you were.

Make a conscious decision to move away from the ego-driven, caged lifestyle of obsessive self seriousness. Search for the new and the fresh in life. Bring humor back into your existence. Notice the wonder of the world around you, practice being spontaneous and, rekindle the magic in your life.

Chapter 7:

Moving to the Next Level

The only way to do great work is to love what you do. -Buddha

Creating a precise image of the best version of yourself is not easy; however, it is essential. You cannot attain a goal that you do not know or cannot visualize. Therefore, take some time to reflect on what the ideal version of yourself looks like. You can holistically assess yourself by examining your strengths, areas of improvement, passions, and values. Spend some time reflecting on the type of person you want to be known as and set up a plan of action to attain your goals. Create a blueprint of yourself and include traits like integrity, positivity, kindness, and humility.

After creating a mental picture of yourself, you can work harder every day, ensuring you are an inch closer to the ideal version of yourself. Establish a plan that will help you form habits that lead to self-improvement. For example, if the ideal version of you involves up-skilling, you can identify and apply for a course, thus increasing your chances of achieving that goal.

You will not achieve the best version of yourself overnight, but you will ultimately get there by taking the necessary steps. Your ideal self is not perfection; it is better than the person you are today. Carefully consider your values and priorities and prepare yourself to build the future that you want on these.

Take some much-needed time to focus on yourself. Be your own best friend and celebrate the unique, talented person that you are. Remember that before anyone else can cherish or celebrate you, you need to value and be your own champion first.

Achieve and experience all the things that you have always wanted to do. Accept and come to the realization that it is not too late for you to dream and achieve your dreams. Spend some time working on your own vulnerabilities so that you can heal and become stronger.

Be your own champion and be a champion for your kids. Make sure that your kids are happy, healthy, and stable.

Goal Setting

"Everything that you do is created twice, once in your mind and then in the physical world." Sounds amazing right? Well, it is. By focusing on our short and long-term goals, you have a greater chance for a better tomorrow. Be courageous, take action, and cultivate a positive mindset so you can manifest your deepest desires.

In the past, you may have tried to take action and set goals but failed to achieve them but do not let this hold you back. From here on out, you will have to do things differently when you take action. This time, taking action will require you to review your past approaches and consider why you may not have achieved your goals.

According to some, the very definition of insanity is doing the same thing repeatedly while expecting a totally different outcome. If you continue to do things the same way that you have always done them, you will get the same result. You have no choice but to start taking action differently to get a different result.

Be mindful of your goals so you can start letting go of the past, upskilling, and reinventing yourself. Your life will change when you start taking practical steps to become more aligned with your core values, priorities, and authentic self rather than the narcissist.

When it comes to setting personal goals, focus on your values and priorities. Start by taking a long, hard look at what really matters to you; and set goals that are aligned with your authentic self.

Choose to focus on what you would love to do or what you have always wanted to do rather than what you think you should do. If you feel like you need help with goal setting, there are therapists and coaches who can give you practical advice.

Next, set realistic and achievable goals. Do not set yourself up for failure by setting goals that require resources you do not have or have no way of getting. It would also be very wise to break down your larger goals into smaller, manageable steps. Remember that most progress will take time and that setbacks are both normal and should be embraced and addressed with a neutral and non-emotional mindset. Remember just to keep going.

Always write down the goals you want to achieve, be specific, and make sure that your goals are measurable. You can do this by setting milestones for your achievements. As you reach certain milestones, celebrate yourself. No matter how small the wins may seem at the time, remember that each success means you are a step closer to achieving your end goal.

Last but not least, your goals need a 'due' date. You need to know exactly how long you are giving yourself to achieve your goal—for instance, six months, one year? Hold yourself accountable when you fall behind on your goals and keep working toward succeeding; your future self will say thank you for not giving up.

Be serious about your plans knowing they are powerful keys that can unlock resilience. You only live once, and at the end of your life, you do not want to look back, regretting everything that you wanted to achieve but did not.

Expanding Horizons

It is never too late for you to rewrite your life story and live a fulfilling and wonderful life. Embrace change with a positive and open mind and watch as you start to transform into the person you have always envisioned becoming!

Change is an entirely normal part of life and be open to it. To live a truly fulfilling life, you want to constantly grow and develop. Choose to be mindful and continually reflect on yourself and your growth. Be aware of the fact that you are taking a decisive step toward enhancing your life by transforming your thoughts, perspective, and actions.

Just like the cycle of change is inevitable, failure and mistakes are part of the learning process and a necessary ingredient for growth.

Reframe and Reinvent Yourself

To reframe and reinvent yourself, take a step back and evaluate exactly where you are now in your life. Take some time to really reflect on your strengths, passions, and areas where you can improve yourself.

Be adventurous, take the time, and explore new and exciting opportunities and experiences that will move your life in the direction you want it to go. This could involve learning new skills, traveling to different places, or meeting new people.

Be open and expand your circle of acquaintances and friends to individuals you resonate with. Talking to those who are already where you want to be will provide you with valuable advice and an already tried and tested framework for achieving your goals.

Find Your Tribe

Each one of us needs to feel as though we belong. Choose to live, learn, grow, and find your tribe. Surround yourself with supportive people who can uplift you and encourage you when needed. You may find your tribe in your town, in meditation groups, or through online platforms.

Discovering and being a part of a community that shares your values and interests is important for developing and feeling like you belong. Connecting with like-minded people who share your beliefs can significantly enhance your spiritual growth and personal development.

When you start to connect with people who share your interests and values, you gain valuable opportunities for learning, mentorship, and meaningful conversations. Finding your tribe will put you in an environment where you feel accepted, inspired, and driven as you embark on a path toward your goals, self-actualization, and inner peace.

The Energy of Different Places

Different places have different energies, and spending time in these places can change your perception of situations. Every location has a unique energy that can impact you in one way or another, whether it's a busy city, a peaceful beach, or a serene mountain.

Cities have their own collective subconscious energy, which can stunt or nurture your growth, depending on how you embrace the place. The coordinated set of behaviors, beliefs, attitudes, and code of conduct expected will affect your energy and behavior as you absorb this. Your own subconscious energy could accept or reject this energy depending on how it fits with your own beliefs and values.

More natural environments like beaches and mountains inspire awe and wonder and may encourage you to slow down and connect with nature. Being in a peaceful environment can make you reflect on yourself and connect more with the universe.

Sacred places like temples, churches, and historical landmarks emit spiritual energy that can invoke feelings of awe, reverence, and connection with a higher power. These settings can help you meditate, reflect, and feel closer to the source of divine energy.

By tapping into the subtler energies of people and places, you can begin to discern where and with whom makes you feel more peaceful and connected.

Work on developing your intuition. Listen to your gut instincts, note down your dreams, and step back when things sound slightly off. Stop and check yourself when you say yes to something that you really want to say no to. Rectify the situation and strengthen your boundaries.

Call-in Your Allies

Visualizations can also help you to call in your allies. By imagining the support of your family, friends, and mentors from wherever they are on the planet, you can create a greater sense of community and belonging that can help you to achieve your goals.

Call in Abundance

The process of calling in abundance visualization involves imagining yourself already having achieved your goal or desire. Create a mental image of yourself with what you want and focus on this image as if it is already a reality. Use positive affirmations and feelings to help bring it to fruition. By focusing on your goal with a positive mindset, you can attract abundance and manifest it in your life.

By consistently visualizing what you want, you are telling the universe what you desire, and the universe will draw more of it toward you. One way to practice visualization is by creating a personal vision board with an inspired collection of images and quotes that represent your goals and desires. By looking at this vision board regularly, you are continuously reminding yourself of what you want, and your mind will focus on making it happen.

Visualization to call in abundance is a simple yet effective technique that even your kids can use to achieve their goals and dreams. Remember to remain consistent and focus on your goal with a positive mindset. Like attracts like, and by focusing on and working toward abundance, you will attract abundance.

Conclusion

In the end, only three things matter: how much you loved, how gently you lived, and how gracefully you let go of things not meant for you. -Gautama Buddha

Once you have kids, life is no longer simple, and not everything is about your needs alone. Suddenly your well-being is not the most important thing in your life. While your kids are most important, looking after yourself will allow you, in turn, to look after them well.

It is awesome that your eyes finally opened, and you realized that you are worth far more than you settled for. Working on creating a new you and a happier life for yourself and your kids is not selfish; it is necessary. Trauma of any kind leaves a deep mark on your soul. However, be encouraged; trauma wounds can heal with time, unconditional self-love, and patience.

Despite what may come your way, always remember that you do matter. You deserve to love and care for yourself from the inside out. After living with a narcissist, it is only normal for your mind to wander to very dark places and for negative emotions to latch onto you at times. It is time to release everything that has been holding you hostage for so long and preventing you from living your best life.

Remember that abuse is not the target's fault and most certainly does not define a person's worth. You deserve to be treated with unconditional love and immeasurable respect, no matter what you have been through in life. It is time for you to rise again and release any guilt and shame that have held you back from healing.

Be wise and choose to surround yourself with people who believe in you and your potential. Do not surround yourself with toxic people who do not support you or who will not encourage you along the way.

Embrace that you are only human and made the mistake of loving someone who really could not love you back. This failed relationship was not all in vain, as you have beautiful kids to embrace every day of your life thanks to the toxic relationship.

Forgive yourself and courageously move forward; we can all make horrible mistakes and decisions in life that we regret later. Ending harmful cycles in our life will make us healthier and happier people who can thrive in life. Instead, failing to put an end to what we knew was a bad situation sooner only makes us feel stupid and regretful. Only when we disrupt the status quo of a negative situation do we realize the full extent of the resistance that was being mounted against us.

Do not neglect self-care; eat a healthy diet, get enough exercise, and sleep are all essential parts of self-care. Take time out to enjoy a bubble bath, read, or listen to music or your favorite podcast. Enjoy hobbies like art or creative pursuits that you enjoy that can give you a healthy outlet for your emotions. Remember that focusing inward is an important part of the healing process.

The techniques that have been outlined in this book are those that I followed in my life, which really gave me the time and space to make tremendous progress. They also gave me a sense of peace and inner calm that had been sadly lacking in my life for over five years due to an accumulation of external noise and chaos that unfolded in front of my eyes across both my private and professional life.

Tuning into the energy around us, discerning what we want to take on, and accepting when we need to impose change are critical to our overall health and well-being. When you catch a glimpse of your ex, perhaps you see flashes of that simmering anger and frustration that had once been dumped onto you as they gleefully wreaked havoc in your life. Now that that anger and frustration are back where it belongs, you can start focusing on living your best life.

Cutting all ties possible and setting and maintaining healthy boundaries while cooperating in the kids' best interests is what has worked best for me. This has also given my kids a strong sense that they are not from a "broken home." While their parents are separated, my kids know their home is not broken but, in fact, functioning.

Set clear boundaries with your ex and ensure they are always respected. Create a written parenting plan and stick to it for your own sanity. When it comes to parenting, always keep it professional; remember that your focus is on your kids' needs, not your own.

Feel empowered, find peaceful solutions where possible, and move forward. Implementing a co-parenting plan founded on your own beliefs and values while understanding the other person's perspective and trying to find compromise is key to that peaceful inner world we must cherish as we walk on this earth.

When you are discussing parenting issues, keep communication as respectful as possible. Do not get involved in silly arguments, personal attacks, or inflammatory statements. Narcissists may try to bait you into a fight, always be alert, and do not engage in this behavior.

Always be prepared for anything that may come your way. Document all communication and decisions made with your narcissistic ex to protect yourself and your kids. If necessary, consult a lawyer so that your legal rights are protected. Maintain perspective at all times and remember that your kids are the most important thing. Under no circumstances should your kids be used as pawns in a conflict between you and your narcissistic co-parent.

While it can be insightful to reflect on your past experiences and choices that you have made, dwelling on your past can be harmful and can also prevent you from moving forward in life. Choose to reframe your past mistakes and use them as powerful opportunities for personal growth and development.

By focusing on self-development, you can achieve your goals and become the very best possible version of yourself. You have the power to shape your own future whichever way you choose to, so refocus your energy on improving yourself and creating a brighter, happier future for you and your kids.

Achieving your dreams and goals is not only rewarding for yourself but for your kids as well. Taking care of yourself and your greatest desires is one of the most valuable gifts you can ever give your kids. Your kids will be far happier and more fulfilled if their mother is happy and fulfilled.

Achieving your heart's desires is a mental, emotional, and practical journey that requires courage, commitment, and a strong sense of self-belief. Anything worth achieving in life requires hard work, determination, patience, perseverance, and sacrifice. By staying focused on what you genuinely want and persevering through challenges, you can achieve your greatest dreams and live the life you have always envisioned. Be a parent who shows their kids that anything they put their minds to is possible.

Challenge yourself to be the best role model possible for your kids and inspire them to strive for greatness. When you set and work toward achieving your goals, you teach your kids the importance of perseverance and determination. Your kids will see and learn the value of hard work and persistence when they see you overcoming challenges and finally reaching your goals.

By achieving your goals, you will instill a sense of great pride and motivation in the hearts and spirits of your kids. This pride and inspiration will then have a ripple effect on your kids and encourage them to work harder toward their dreams. You can and will be a parent who shows your kids that anything they put their minds to is possible.

Embrace the brighter side of life, have fun and be adventurous. Try new activities, meet new people, explore, grow and learn. Be spontaneous and look for the magic in life.

Be inspired; great things lie ahead of you. The incredible journey that you are about to embark on may seem like a massive unclimbable mountain in front of you, but you can do this. Once you discover new, improved versions of yourself, you will be grateful that you were courageous enough to take steps toward self-discovery.

Glossary

Abundance: A state of having an excess or overflow of something. It can refer to material things, finances, emotional fulfillment, and even time. Abundance refers to having more than enough of what you want and need in life. It is not just about wealth or material things but also the satisfaction of having truly meaningful relationships, good health, personal growth, and enriching experiences.

Affirmations: A positive statement used to help build your self-esteem and confidence. Affirmations can help you stay focused on goals and stay positive despite difficult situations.

Allies: People or groups that come together to support a common goal. These people will offer assistance, resources, and advocacy in times of hardship and need.

Bonding: The process of creating a close relationship between two people, whether it's friends, family members, or romantic partners. Bonding involves sharing experiences and emotions, developing trust and understanding, and creating a true sense of belonging.

Boundaries: Guidelines, rules, or limits you set to identify safe, reasonable, and permissible ways for others to behave toward you.

Child Support: Financial support paid by one parent to the other parent toward their child's upbringing. This is generally paid by the parent who does not have primary custody of the child and is usually ordered by the court.

Consistency: Being reliable and predictable by maintaining a consistent approach in actions, behavior, and performance.

Co-parenting: The arrangement in which parents who no longer live together cooperate to raise their kids.

Co-parenting Plan: A written agreement between two parents outlining the parenting plan over a period of time.

Communication: The exchange of information, ideas, and thoughts. The exchange of thoughts, messages, or information, as by speech, signals, writing, or behavior.

Compromise: A settlement of differences where each person makes concessions.

Conscious Parenting: Also known as active parenting, it is a unique parenting style that emphasizes the importance of actively parenting kids while striving to be mindful of their individual needs, feelings, and perspectives. Conscious parenting emphasizes the importance of open communication, mutual respect, and positive reinforcement while seeking to develop strong relationships with one's kids.

Conflict Resolution: The process of resolving a dispute or disagreement, usually through discussion.

Cooperation: A situation in which two or more people or groups work together intending to achieve a common goal.

Coping Strategies: Techniques individuals use to manage difficult emotions or stressful situations.

Discernment: The ability to judge well and make good decisions based on careful consideration, knowledge, and insight.

Dysfunctional Patterns: Dysfunctional patterns are the behaviors, thoughts, and emotions that tend to cause distress and interfere with an individual's ability to function effectively in their daily life. Dysfunctional patterns can manifest in various ways, including anxiety, depression, anger, and avoidance.

Effective Communication: A powerful tool in interpersonal interactions that involves actively listening to what someone is saying, understanding their message, and responding thoughtfully. This type of communication can be achieved through both verbal and non-verbal means and requires being mindful of your audience's needs and using empathy to connect with them.

Ego: The ego is a term used to describe the self or sense of identity we all possess. It makes you unique with your beliefs, feelings, and thoughts. Essentially, the ego is the part of yourself that distinguishes us from others and keeps us grounded in our individuality.

Emotional Distancing: Creating an emotional barrier between oneself and another person or situation. It can involve withdrawing attention, avoiding physical or verbal contact, and suppressing feelings of attachment, empathy, or intimacy. Emotional distancing can be used as a coping mechanism to protect oneself from being emotionally overwhelmed or hurt.

Emotional Management Techniques: Skills and strategies that can help you understand, control, and express your emotions well. These include mindfulness, deep breathing, and self-reflection practices.

Emotional Ties: The strong feelings of connection that bind two people together. These ties can be based on love, loyalty, trust, or shared experiences, both positive and negative. Close connections, often based on shared experiences that form between two or more people, usually family members, and create a bond. In a co-parenting context, emotional ties can be a source of both comfort and stress, as they involve a connection to the other parent that cannot easily be severed.

Emotions: A combination of physical sensations, thoughts, and actions that are shaped by personal experiences.

Empathy: Understanding what another person is experiencing from their point of view. Also, the ability to recognize and understand the feelings of other people. Empathy requires a deep level of emotional intelligence and sensitivity toward others. It involves:

- Actively listening to what someone says.

- Paying attention to their nonverbal cues.

- Acknowledging their emotions without judgment or criticism.

Financial Ties: Ongoing financial transactions or support between entities, such as investments, loans, partnerships, donations, and other forms of exchange. When co-parenting with a narcissistic partner, financial ties involve the non-narcissistic co-parent's obligation to provide financial support, like child support or alimony.

Fixed Mindset: A fixed mindset is the belief that abilities and intelligence are unchangeable traits that cannot be developed further.

Forgiveness: A choice to intentionally let go of negative emotions such as anger, resentment, or the desire for revenge toward someone who has wronged us. It involves acknowledging that we cannot change the past and consciously releasing these negative feelings for our own well-being.

Gaslighting: a form of manipulation in which people or groups sow seeds of doubt at a targeted individual or group, making them question their own memory, perception, or judgment. Using persistent denial, misdirection, contradiction, and lying, gaslighting can destabilize the target and delegitimize the target's belief.

Goals: The things we want to achieve in different areas of our lives. They help us focus and give us direction. They act like a map for our actions and decisions.

Growth Mindset: If you have a growth mindset, you view challenges as opportunities to improve yourself. By working hard and staying committed, you can develop your abilities.

Healing: The process of recovering from any illness, injury, or emotional trauma. Healing is usually profoundly personal and involves restoring health and vitality to the mind, body, and spirit. Healing is not limited to physical recovery but also mental and spiritual aspects necessary for complete well-being.

Joint Custody: A form of child custody wherein both parents have legal custody of their kids, regardless of where the child lives.

Journaling: Putting pen to paper (or fingers to keyboard) and pouring out your thoughts, emotions, and experiences.

Legal Representation: Representation of a party in court by an attorney.

Love languages: A concept that helps us understand how people show and receive love. There are five main love languages which are words of affirmation, acts of service, receiving gifts, quality time, and physical touch.

Mantra: Tool for the mind. A Mantra is a powerful phrase or word often used in meditation, which is repeated to aid concentration and bring about a state of calm and peace. It is believed that mantras can transform the mind and body.

Mediation: A form of dispute resolution where an unbiased third party (the mediator) facilitates communication between people to promote reconciliation, settlement, or understanding. Also, a process in which two or more parties try to reach an agreement without involving a court.

Meditation: A focused relaxation and stillness practice, often used to reduce stress and increase self-awareness. It is a powerful tool to cultivate calm, clarity, and balance amid difficult situations. It can also help to cultivate the ability to remain present and non-reactive in the face of difficult emotions and challenging conversations.

Mental Health Professionals: Trained and licensed practitioners specializing in mental health treatment. These include psychologists, psychiatrists, social workers, counselors, and therapists. They work across various settings, including hospitals, clinics, schools, and private practice - using multiple techniques, including psychodynamic or cognitive behavioral therapy.

Mindset: Your mindset is your mental attitude and influences how you think, behave, and react in different areas of life. It affects how you see situations, make decisions, and determines your personal growth and success. This includes your beliefs, values, attitudes, and assumptions that are ingrained in your subconscious mind.

Mutual Problem-Solving: The collaborative approach that people or groups take to identify and resolve issues or challenges that impact them collectively. This involves all parties working together toward a common goal, exchanging ideas, perspectives, and expertise.

Narcissism: A personality disorder characterized by a toxic pattern of grandiosity, lack of empathy, and an excessive need for admiration.

Narcissist: A person who lacks empathy for other people, has an insatiable need for admiration, and an inflated sense of self-importance.

Narcissistic Personality Therapy: A type of psychotherapy that focuses on helping individuals with narcissistic personality disorder to better understand their own behavior and improve their relationships with others.

Neuroplasticity: The human brain's ability to rewire or restructure itself.

Parental Alienation: A form of psychological abuse in which a child is manipulated or influenced by one parent to unjustifiably reject or show hostility toward the other parent.

Parental Alienation Syndrome (PAS): When a child expresses unjustified hatred or unreasonably strong negative feelings toward one parent, which is influenced by the other parent.

Parenting: Nurturing and guiding a child as they navigate their way through life.

Parenting Style: The approach a parent takes in raising a child, which may include elements such as discipline, communication, and warm involvement. Parenting styles can range from highly authoritarian to highly permissive and may be based on a child's age, maturity level, and individual needs.

Physical Ties: Connections that exist between people, often in the form of a relationship, such as a marriage or friendship. These ties can be strengthened through physical contact, shared experiences, and emotional support. Physical ties are the relationships a co-parent with a narcissist has with one another through their kids. This includes the emotional, spiritual, and financial support each parent provides their kids.

Resilience: Ability to recover quickly from difficulties; toughness. It is the ability to adapt to or cope with difficult conditions. It is the strength and flexibility to withstand and quickly recover from difficult situations.

Self-Discovery: The process of gaining a deep understanding and awareness of oneself. It is an introspective journey that involves exploring one's values, beliefs, strengths, weaknesses, desires, and emotions.

Self-Help: Working on your personal growth, development, and well-being through your own actions and efforts. You can do this by seeking advice, information, and strategies from various sources like books, workshops, videos, or online resources. Through self-help, you can improve yourself mentally, emotionally, physically, or spiritually.

Spiritual Cord: A spiritual cord connects two people who have a close relationship or deep emotional bond. It's like an energetic string that symbolizes a strong bond between them on a deeper level. It allows them to feel each other's emotions and energy, creating a telepathic-like connection. Some believe the cord can affect their thoughts and feelings even if they are physically apart.

Support: Helping someone achieve their goals and overcome obstacles. It can be emotional, practical, or just listening. People can get support from friends, family, mentors, and counselors.

Therapy: A treatment or set of treatments, usually involving counseling or other psychological techniques, intended to improve a person's mental or physical condition.

Visualization: A mental image or representation of an idea, situation, or object. Visualization is often used as a meditation and mindfulness tool and can help bring focus and clarity to a situation.

Volunteering: Helping others without expecting anything in return.

Yoga: A practice that combines physical movement, breath control, and meditation to promote relaxation, flexibility, and overall well-being. It originated in ancient India and has evolved into various styles over thousands of years. Yoga is about more than just impressive poses on a mat; it focuses on the connection between the mind, body, and spirit.

Your Tribe: A community that shares similar beliefs, practices, and values where you can seek companionship and support on the spiritual journey toward enlightenment.

References

Admin, & Hospital, W. P. (2018, September 18). Health Matters Blog | White Plains Hospital Healthcare Information. WP Hospital. https://healthmatters.wphospital.org/blog/september/2018/the-armonk-outdoor-art-show/

American Psychological Association. (2017). *Eye Movement Desensitization and Reprocessing (EMDR) Therapy*. American Psychological Association. https://www.apa.org/ptsd-guideline/treatments/eye-movement-reprocessing

Arain, M., Mathur, P., Rais, A., Nel, W., Sandhu, R., Haque, M., Johal, L., & Sharma, S. (2013). *Maturation of the Adolescent Brain*. Neuropsychiatric Disease and Treatment, 9(9), 449–461. https://doi.org/10.2147/ndt.s39776

Breazeale, R. (2017, May 2). *S.M.A.R.T. Goals* | Psychology Today South Africa. Www.psychologytoday.com; Psychology Today. https://www.psychologytoday.com/za/blog/in-the-face-adversity/201705/smart-goals

Buddha, G. (n.d.). *A quote by Gautama Buddha*. Www.goodreads.com. Retrieved June 11, 2023, from https://www.goodreads.com/quotes/3181192-in-the-end-only-three-things-matter-how-much-you

Buddha. (n.d.). *The Big Book of Gautama Buddha Quotes*. Goodreads; Goodreads. Retrieved June 16, 2023, from https://www.goodreads.com/book/show/126113503-the-big-book-of-gautama-buddha-quotes

Buddha. (n.d.). *A quote by Budha*. Www.goodreads.com; Good Reads. Retrieved June 9, 2023, from https://www.goodreads.com/quotes/632288-the-mind-is-everything-what-you-think-you-become

Buddha. (n.d.-a). *A quote by Budha.* Www.goodreads.com; GoodReads. Retrieved May 31, 2023, from https://www.goodreads.com/quotes/632288-the-mind-is-everything-what-you-think-you-become

Buddha. (n.d.-b). *A quote from 600 Quotes of Ancient Philosophy.* Www.goodreads.com; GoodReads. Retrieved May 31, 2023, from https://www.goodreads.com/quotes/11364593-you-yourself-as-much-as-anybody-in-the-entire-universe

Burchard, B. (n.d.). *Clean Slate Quotes* (6 quotes). Www.goodreads.com; GoodReads. Retrieved May 1, 2023, from https://www.goodreads.com/quotes/tag/clean-slate

Cleveland Clinic. (2014). *Narcissistic Personality Disorder | Cleveland Clinic.* Cleveland Clinic; Cleveland Clinic. https://my.clevelandclinic.org/health/diseases/9742-narcissistic-personality-disorder

Cox, J. (2017, November 13). *What Is a Narcissistic Personality and Can It Be Treated?* Psych Central. https://psychcentral.com/disorders/narcissistic-personality-disorder#takeaway

Crider, C. (2020, April 24). *What Is Conscious Parenting? Key Points, Benefits, and Drawbacks.* Healthline. https://www.healthline.com/health/parenting/conscious-parenting#takeaway

Duncan, A. (2022, November 2). *Life Skills to Start Teaching Your Kids at an Early Age.* Verywell Family. https://www.verywellfamily.com/teaching-children-life-skills-early-4144959

Eddy, B. (2018, September 30). *BIFF: 4 Ways to Respond to Hostile Comments | Psychology Today South Africa.* Www.psychologytoday.com; Psychology Today. https://www.psychologytoday.com/za/blog/5-types-people-who-can-ruin-your-life/201809/biff-4-ways-respond-hostile-comments

Funke, C. (n.d.). *A quote from Inkheart.* Www.goodreads.com; GoodReads. Retrieved May 31, 2023, from https://www.goodreads.com/quotes/8141801-a-thousand-enemies-outside-the-house-are-better-than-one

Hanh, T. N. (n.d.). Thich Nhat Hanh Quote: *"The most precious inheritance that parents can give their children is their own happiness."* Quotefancy.com; Quote Fancy. Retrieved June 9, 2023, from https://quotefancy.com/quote/1998378/Thich-Nhat-Hanh-The-most-precious-inheritance-that-parents-can-give-their-children-is

Hochenberger, K. L. (2021, March 26). *Can't Buy Me Love: Narcissists and Financial Abuse* | Psychology Today South Africa. Www.psychologytoday.com; Psychology Today. https://www.psychologytoday.com/za/blog/love-in-the-age-narcissism/202103/can-t-buy-me-love-narcissists-and-financial-abuse

Horton, L. (2019, August 8). *The Neuroscience Behind Our Words.* BRM Institute. https://brm.institute/neuroscience-behind-words/

Li, P. (2019, November 5). *Resilience in Children, Resilience Factors and Examples.* Parenting for Brain. https://www.parentingforbrain.com/resilience/#:~:text=Strengthening%20the%20protective%20factors%20to

Malone, T. (n.d.). *Coparenting Quotes* (6 quotes). Www.goodreads.com; GoodReads. Retrieved May 1, 2023, from https://www.goodreads.com/quotes/tag/coparenting#:~:text=%E2%80%9CIf%20you%20hold%20onto%20hurt

Miller, R. (2015, May 27). *Raising Non-Violent Children: A Survivor's Perspective.* See the Triumph. http://www.seethetriumph.org/blog/raising-non-violent-children-a-survivors-perspective

Mohsin, H. (2022, May 27). *World Narcissistic Abuse Day.* National Today. https://nationaltoday.com/world-narcissistic-abuse-day/

Northern Exposure, Season 3 Quotes. (n.d.). Quotes.net. Retrieved May 18, 2023, from https://www.quotes.net/show-quote/60892.

Raypole, C. (2020, June 17). *How to Rewire Your Brain: 6 Neuroplasticity Exercises.* Healthline. https://www.healthline.com/health/rewiring-your-brain

Rogers, S. L., Howieson, J., & Neame, C. (2018). *I understand you feel that way, but I feel this way: the benefits of I-language and communicating perspective during conflict.* PeerJ, 6, e4831. https://doi.org/10.7717/peerj.4831

Rosen, P. (n.d.). *Emotional Intelligence in Children | LD, ADHD and Emotional Skills.* Www.understood.org. Retrieved May 30, 2023, from https://www.understood.org/en/articles/the-importance-of-emotional-intelligence-for-kids-with-learning-and-thinking-differences

Sanvictores, T., & Mendez, M. D. (2022, September 18). *Types of Parenting Styles and Effects On Children.* PubMed; StatPearls Publishing. https://www.ncbi.nlm.nih.gov/books/NBK568743/

Tsabary, S. (n.d.). *The Conscious Parent Quotes by Shefali Tsabary.* Www.goodreads.com; GoodReads. Retrieved May 31, 2023, from https://www.goodreads.com/work/quotes/7361869-the-conscious-parent

van Schie, C. C., Jarman, H. L., Huxley, E., & Grenyer, B. F. S. (2020). *Narcissistic traits in young people: understanding the role of parenting and maltreatment.* Borderline Personality Disorder and Emotion Dysregulation, 7(1). https://doi.org/10.1186/s40479-020-00125-7

World Health Organization. (2022, September 19). *Child Maltreatment.* Who.int; World Health Organization: WHO. https://www.who.int/news-room/fact-sheets/detail/child-maltreatment/

Made in United States
North Haven, CT
30 January 2024

48098543R00070